THE TRUTH DETECTIVE

In loving memory of Adrian and Deb Harford

First published in Great Britain in 2023 by Wren & Rook

ISBN: 978 1 5263 6457 9
E-book ISBN: 978 1 5263 6458 6

1 3 5 7 9 10 8 6 4 2

Wren & Rook
An imprint of
Hachette Children's Group
Part of Hodder & Stoughton
Carmelite House
50 Victoria Embankment
London EC4Y 0DZ

An Hachette UK Company
www.hachette.co.uk
www.hachettechildrens.co.uk

Printed in China

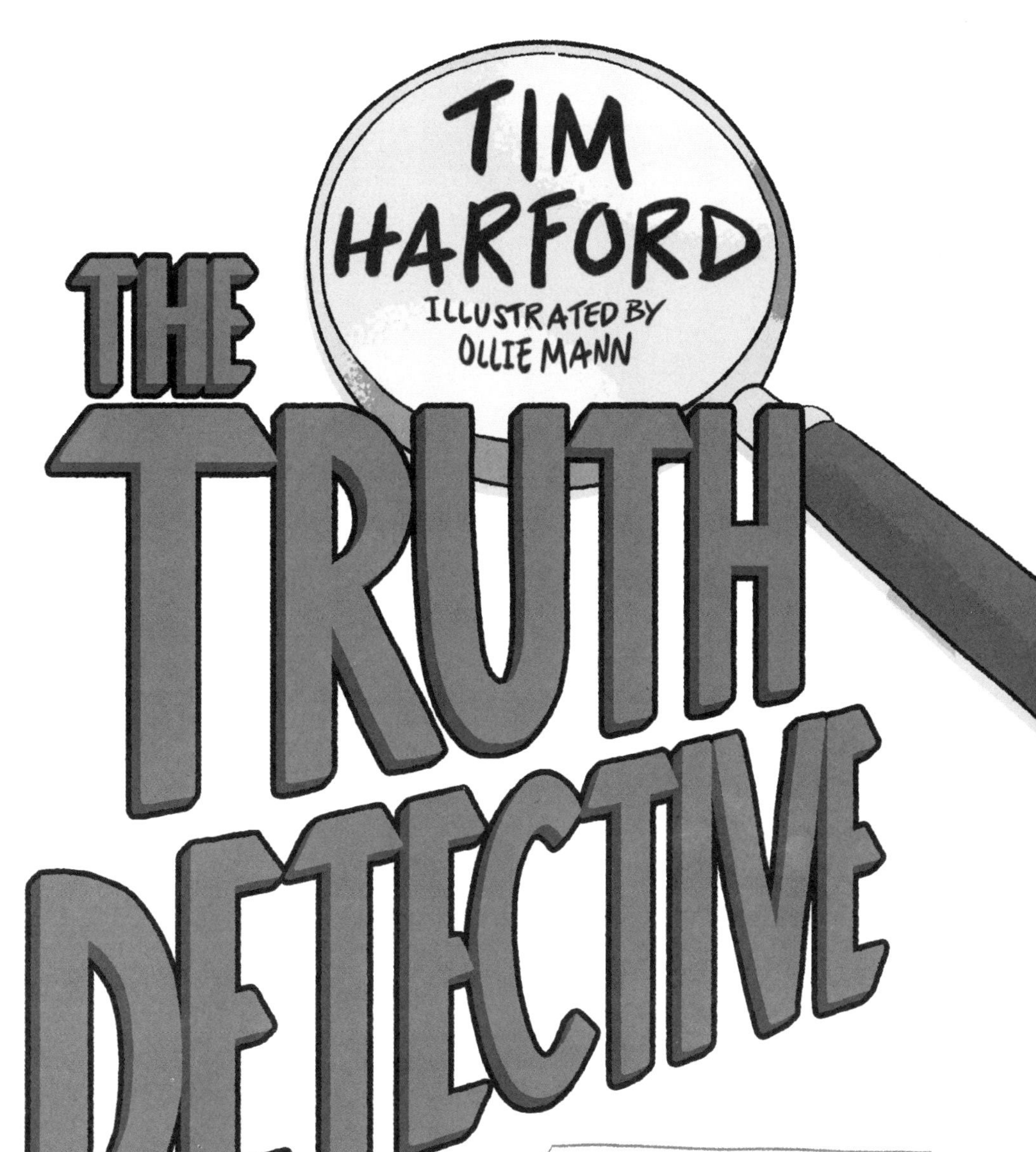

HOW TO MAKE
SENSE OF A WORLD
THAT DOESN'T ADD UP

CONTENTS

SECTION TWO: THE SKILLS OF A TRUTH DETECTIVE

SECTION THREE: HOW TO CRACK DIFFICULT CASES

Introduction: Get Your Gear

This is a book about how to think clearly about the world. You obviously think clearly already, because you've made the smart decision to pick it up. But I hope this book will help you to be even smarter.

The world can be a confusing place. People say a lot of things that seem true, but aren't. And sometimes they say things that feel like they can't be true – but they are.

Our job here is to figure out what is TRUE and what is NOT – like a detective. But instead of catching the murderer or cracking the code, a Truth Detective is hunting for the truth.

The truth about what? The truth about cases such as this:

- **What do you do if your parents think Minecraft is leading you into a life of crime?**

- **How can a pooping cow see into the future?**

- **How much pocket money is a lot?**
- **What's better, a T-Rex standing next to a bus or a pile of money stretching into space?**
- **What should you think if someone shows you a photograph of a dancing fairy?**

But finding the truth isn't easy. Even the cleverest people can be fooled. (If you don't believe me, read on to discover a blunder from the creator of Sherlock Holmes, the most famous fictional detective of all.)[1] There are many ways in which the truth can be concealed, and there are dastardly masterminds desperate to do just that. (This book will help you spot them.)

HEROES AND VILLAINS

Throughout this book we'll be meeting some truth detective heroes and villains. Some are from storybooks or films; others are very real indeed. Pay close attention to what they say and do – you'll need to pay attention to outsmart the villains, and there's a lot to learn from the heroes if you stay alert!

---

[1] *I think Holmes is my favourite detective – although that may be because I first saw Sherlock Holmes on a TV show in which he was being played by the actor who ALSO played Doctor Who. So I got Sherlock Holmes and Doctor Who a bit confused in my mind – in a good way . . .*

TRUTH DETECTIVE

DARTH VADER

Our first truth detective hero is . . . DARTH VADER, Lord of the Sith, from the *Star Wars* movies. He might seem a strange hero, since he is one of the scariest enemies in cinema. But even the bad guy can give good advice, and Darth Vader does give a very good piece of advice to Luke Skywalker: '*Search your feelings.*' Our feelings often determine what we believe and what we refuse to believe. This book will give you lots of skills and ideas to help you figure out what's true – but if you don't keep an eye on your own feelings, and notice when they are affecting you, those skills and ideas will be in vain.

Luckily, the quest to figure out what's true is fun. You won't need complicated mathematics. In fact, **THE TEN SIMPLE RULES IN THIS BOOK** will have you finding clues and solving tough cases MUCH BETTER THAN MOST GROWN-UPS. And you'll have lots of friends to help you along the way – some pretty awesome people have walked the same path ahead of you. We'll meet some of them as we go. So shall we get started?

Choose Your Detective Kit

Lots of famous detectives from films, books and TV shows have their own distinctive look. Let's meet them, and try on some of their famous disguises.

HERCULE POIROT, the Belgian detective, wears a rather natty moustache – but of course that's not for everyone. Good for twirling, though.

BROTHER CADFAEL is a monk–detective, which means he wears a hood (cool), a long woollen thing called a habit (not so cool) and shaves a little bald patch on the top of his head (definitely an unusual choice).

And you can't get more distinctive than **BATMAN** – the brooding, mysterious scourge of the criminal underworld.[2] He has a cape, a mask, a utility belt, a bat-boomerang called a 'batarang' and the Batmobile. He also sometimes wears underpants over the top of his outfit. He's fully committed to his look.

---

[2] *If you're thinking that Batman is a superhero rather than a detective, he's both. The first Batman story was published in Detective Comics.*

Of course, you could combine different elements of these outfits – perhaps a shaved head, a twirly moustache and visible underpants? But that might attract too much attention.

You might prefer to stay beneath the radar and be an

UNDERCOVER TRUTH DETECTIVE

Consider **VERONICA MARS**. She's a private investigator who looks – well, exactly like what she is, which is a teenager who spends most of her time at an American high school.

Or **FELUDA**, a private investigator from Bengal, India. Feluda is so famous in India that a test for coronavirus was named after him, but he doesn't look unusual: he's tall but quiet. He hides his brilliant brain behind an ordinary-looking face.

OTTOLINE BROWN is a mistress of disguise – in fact, she even has a diploma from the Who-R-U Academy of Disguise. She is a refined young woman who appears exactly as she wishes to appear. (Like many detectives, Ottoline has a sidekick. Unlike most, her sidekick, Mr Munroe, looks like a mop.)

MISS MARPLE is a little old lady. She doesn't have a twirly moustache and she doesn't have a Batmobile. Nobody ever sees HER underpants. People often take old ladies for granted, which means that Miss Marple is underestimated by her enemies. (That's my excuse for wearing jeans and a cardigan and looking like a dork. The truth is I'm just trying to get my enemies to underestimate me, too.)

There are plenty of other detectives out there and you could take inspiration from any one of them. But when it comes to being a Truth Detective, you don't need special equipment like Batman or even an elaborate hairdo like Cadfael.

So . . . what do you need? A magnifying glass? Fingerprint powder?

No. First you need **DATA**. You might already know that data is a fancy word for, well, numbers. Being smart and savvy about numbers helps you to be smart and savvy about everything. In chapter two, we'll come back to why numbers are such an important tool for understanding the world.

For now, just know that even if you don't think you want to chase after numbers, the numbers are chasing after you. That's right, they've escaped from maths class and they're everywhere! The news websites are full of numbers, whether it's politicians boasting about how great they are or scary stories about crime, accidents or diseases. Social media is full of numbers, too: every post we look at lists likes or shares.

Sometimes it seems like we're more interested in the numbers underneath the post than what it actually says. Even when we don't see the numbers, they shape our world. Who decides what

to show you next on YouTube or TikTok? It's not a human being making recommendations. It's the numbers – complex, hidden calculations based on everyone else's viewing habits, aiming to show you something that will keep you scrolling and watching.

Numbers are all around us, and you're going to need to understand them if you want to crack difficult cases. What sort of cases? We've heard about some already.

Here are some more:

- **What's the best way to stop a plane from being shot down?**
- **What's the key to understanding how people survive in terrible poverty?**
- **How rich are the richest people on the planet?**
- **Can pictures save lives? Can numbers? What about pictures of numbers?**

But the tips in this book should help you be smarter about thinking through . . . well, almost anything. And while numbers are an important tool for discovering clues, this isn't a book about maths. You don't need to be good at maths to enjoy it (phew!), because the tricks that we need if we're going to think clearly about numbers aren't special mathematical methods. They're ideas and tactics that anyone can learn – including you!

TRICKS, TACTICS AND TOOLS

Truth Detectives come in all shapes and sizes. Some have a distinctive look (Cadfael, Poirot) and some disguise their identities (Ottoline, Batman), but many of the most effective ones look completely ordinary (Feluda, Miss Marple, Veronica Mars). It's what's on the inside that counts – not your costume or your gear. So the tools we'll collect along the way are mental tools – ideas, strategies and hacks that will help you solve difficult cases, avoid mistakes and outsmart the TRUTH VILLAINS. Batman stores gadgets in his utility belt. Miss Marple keeps everything she needs in her handbag. But you? You're going to keep these mental tools tucked away in your head. And here are three essential ideas to start:

TRICKS, TACTICS AND TOOLS

1) The first is data – that is, numbers. They are everywhere, measuring and counting and influencing our world. If you want to get to the truth, you have to get comfortable with numbers – data can provide vital clues!
2) Second, you need to use your brain. Being a good Truth Detective isn't about carrying out a complicated mathematical procedure. A lot of it is about being thoughtful, imaginative and willing to look beyond the obvious.
3) Most important of all is the right attitude. Without that, the smartest people with the deepest knowledge can be very, very wrong . . . as we'll discover.

So let's start with the attitude. A lot of people think you need to be smart to figure out what's true and what's not. Maybe. But I think it's even more important to keep your cool. To understand why, let's try to crack our very first case – and the most famous detective of all, Sherlock Holmes, will be along for the ride.

SECTION ONE

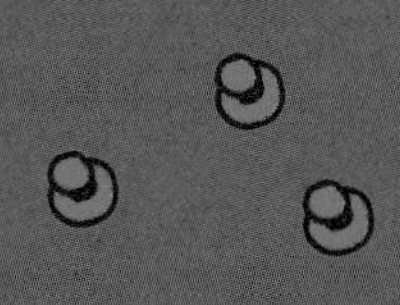

THE TRUTH DETECTIVE MINDSET

DON'T FOOL YOURSELF

The Curious Case of the Cottingley Fairies

About a hundred years ago, a famous writer named Arthur received a very surprising letter. The letter explained to Arthur that a strange and wonderful thing had happened: two little girls from Yorkshire in the north of England had **PHOTOGRAPHED FAIRIES** at the bottom of their garden.

Arthur took a look at the photograph. It was beautiful: a nine-year-old girl (her name was Frances) smiled into the camera, surrounded by four tiny women with wings. Her cousin Elsie had taken the photograph. Arthur wrote a book explaining that this was either the 'most elaborate and ingenious hoax' or an event that would redefine human history.

So . . . you're the Truth Detective. Fairies? Or a trick, a 'hoax'? You get to decide.

These are old-fashioned photographs, from long before you could take a photo on your phone and use an app to edit it. Faking photographs would mean actually painting on to the image itself with a paintbrush or doing some other complicated trick. It is hard to believe that two little girls were able to pull off trick photography.

But it is also hard to believe in fairies at the bottom of the garden. So did these girls really photograph spirits from a magical world, or were the photographs faked?

We need to find some clues. The great detective Sherlock Holmes explained his method of 'observation and deduction' – that is, LOOK for clues and then THINK.

OBSERVATION: Nobody except Frances and Elsie ever saw fairies. The pictures were always made when adults weren't around.

DEDUCTION: Maybe fairies are shy – or maybe they don't exist.

OBSERVATION: Photography experts thought the photographs were faked, but they weren't sure how.

DEDUCTION: Perhaps the experts were confused by fairy magic, but more likely the photos are a trick.

OBSERVATION: Because these were the early days of photography, anything that moved would look fuzzy and blurred in the picture. In the photograph of Frances with the dancing fairies, a waterfall behind her is completely blurred, but the dancing fairies are clear and sharp.

DEDUCTION: The fairies weren't moving, which suggests that they were paper cut-outs, or were painted on to the photograph later.

OBSERVATION: Frances's cousin Elsie wasn't a nine-year-old girl. She was sixteen. Elsie studied art. Her teacher said she was very clever at drawing and cutting out pictures of fairies. She also had a job working in a photography studio . . . altering photographs after they had been taken.

DEDUCTION: Elsie had the technical skill to fake the photographs.

Those are the clues. So . . . what do you suspect? It seems pretty likely that the photographs were faked, right? The circumstances were suspicious, the photographs show clear signs of being faked and even though Elsie was young, she was pretty awesome at art, and it was LITERALLY HER JOB TO ALTER PHOTOGRAPHS.

If that's what you think, I agree. But Arthur did not. He had no doubt that the fairies were real, and he was so sure of it that he said so in his book. How strange.

What makes it even stranger is that this Arthur was Sir Arthur

Conan Doyle, the author of the Sherlock Holmes books! Sherlock Holmes is the perfect symbol of brilliant logic, the most famous detective ever imagined. What Harry Potter is for wizards or Superman is for superheroes, Sherlock Holmes is for detectives. And it was Sir Arthur who created Sherlock Holmes. Sir Arthur was also an expert photographer! And yet a couple of children fooled him into believing in fairies.

How did this happen? And what does it teach us about being a Truth Detective?

Well, Sir Arthur let his own emotions fool him. You see, Sir Arthur was feeling sad. His wife had died young. In the great flu epidemic of 1918, his brother had died too. So had his oldest son. He didn't want these people to be dead. So – what if they weren't *completely* dead? What if they lived on in the spirit world, still watching him, and perhaps still able to talk if he could find the right way? (These beliefs about speaking to spirits sound strange to us now, but they were popular ideas at the time.)

For Sir Arthur, fairies meant something about the family he loved and had lost. Missing his wife and his brother and his son, Sir Arthur was looking for evidence that there is much more to life than we can see and touch. The fairy photographs were that evidence. So Sir Arthur really, really *wanted* to believe in fairies.

But do people believe strange things just because they want them to be true? I would like to have superpowers – perhaps you would too.[3] But just because you want something to be true doesn't mean you think it's true. I don't actually think I can turn myself invisible (and if I did think that, I would be in trouble pretty quick). But Sir Arthur *did* believe in fairies because he wanted to. So how and why did he do that? I blame the Brain Guard.

---

[3] *What superpower would you really like to have? Flight? Invisibility? The ability to shoot death rays from your eyes? There must be something.*

The Brain Guard

Yes, it's time to meet something I call the Brain Guard.

The Brain Guard is like a passport control officer or a security guard. The guard decides who is allowed in and who isn't. Someone comes along asking to be let in, and the guard considers the evidence. The guard should get all the facts, and maybe look at their passport or identification, before deciding. But actually that's not how the guard works. Instead, often the guard looks people up and down – checks out their shoes, their clothes, their hair – and decides whether they *fit* or not.

If they don't look right, the guard sends them away.

If that sounds weird and unfair – well, yes, it is.

The Brain Guard is a security guard not for a building or a country, but for your brain. New ideas, new stories and new facts come along, hoping to be let into your brain – but the Brain Guard is there, looking them up and down, asking if they fit or not. All of us have a Brain Guard – and all of us should pay more attention to what it is doing. Why? Because, like a real-world security guard, our Brain Guard doesn't always get it right.

So what questions would you want the Brain Guard to ask? Here are a few:

- **Does this idea make sense?**
- **Does this story conflict with something I already know to be true?**
- **Does the fact come from a trustworthy source?**

WHAT IS A TRUSTWORTHY SOURCE?

That is a big and difficult question. Nothing is totally trustworthy – you always have to think for yourself. But if I see a claim in an encyclopaedia or a textbook, I would usually take that seriously. A well-known news website is probably accurate, but anyone can post any nonsense on TikTok or Facebook. Yet some news stories on well-known websites are wrong and some posts on social media are absolutely correct.

You can trust different people on different subjects: for example, I trust a newspaper or TV news to tell me what politicians are saying and doing. But I wouldn't necessarily trust them to get everything right about science, because journalists aren't trained scientists. I would trust what my maths teacher tells me about maths, but I might not trust them to advise me about what music is cool.

If the answer to those questions is 'yes', maybe the idea should be allowed into your brain.

What about these questions?

- **Does the person telling me this fact seem friendly and confident?**
- **Do I *want* this idea to be true?**
- **Does this story make me feel something, like fear or joy?**
- **Is this a cool story?**

These questions aren't a great way for a Truth Detective to solve a case. Whether a story is cool, or the storyteller is confident, has nothing to do with truth and lies.

But I'm afraid they are the questions your Brain Guard often asks. The Brain Guard is emotional, a bit lazy and relies on first impressions. The Brain Guard likes ideas that are simple and exciting. It makes superficial judgements ('the person who told me this *seems* nice') and it is a real wishful thinker. Your Brain Guard invites in lots of ideas that don't make much sense, because they feel good or exciting. Sometimes it invites in ideas that are scary, because it's hard to ignore scary ideas. And the Brain Guard sends away lots of ideas that should be allowed in,

because they feel annoying or complicated or just wrong.

So . . . what did Sir Arthur Conan Doyle's Brain Guard do with the clues that arrived?

Clue: Nobody except Frances and Elsie ever saw fairies. Doesn't that suggest the fairies are fake?

Brain Guard: Nope. Fairies are probably real but they're rarely seen. They must be shy.

Clue: Photography experts thought the photographs were faked . . .

Brain Guard: Really? That's impossible. These were little girls. They could never fake the photographs.

Clue: . . . but the experts aren't sure how.

Brain Guard: Oh, that's more interesting. So the experts are confused, are they? Must be confused by fairy magic.

Clue: Because these were the early days of photography, anything that moved would look very blurred in the picture. In the photograph of Frances with the dancing fairies, a waterfall behind her is completely blurred, but the dancing fairies are clear and sharp.

Brain Guard: What I'm hearing is 'blah blah blah, the dancing fairies are clear and sharp'. Excellent – so you say these are high-quality photographs?

MODIFIED CLUE ADMITTED.

Clue: Frances's cousin Elsie studied art . . .

Brain Guard: Let me stop you right there. Who cares what Elsie studied? I think we should let these beautiful photographs speak for themselves.

The Brain Guard is a strange thing, isn't it? And Sir Arthur's Brain Guard did him no favours. It eagerly welcomed some information – for example, the pictures were sharp and the experts didn't know how they were taken – but it rejected important facts, such as that the experts thought the photographs were fake, and that one of the 'children' was actually a teenager with training as an artist and a job in a photography studio.

This process of rejecting some facts and accepting others, depending on what we want or expect to see, is what psychologists (people who study how the mind works) call **CONFIRMATION BIAS**. But you can imagine it as the lazy, superficial Brain Guard at work.

If you're to become a serious Truth Detective – more like Sherlock Holmes, less like Sir Arthur Conan Doyle – you'll have to get your Brain Guard under control. Here's the secret . . .

. . . are you ready? . . .
. . . NOTICE HOW YOU ARE FEELING.
(It's Darth Vader's rule!)

When you see a new idea, what you believe isn't just about how the facts fit together. It's about emotions. You may feel angry, or joyful, or sad, or afraid because of something you see on the internet, read in a book, see in the news or hear from a friend.

All school dinners will be served with extra-soggy cabbage?

Free chocolate for everyone who clicks on this link?

The best band in the world are rumoured to be splitting up?

Stop
TRUTH HERE
WATCH OUT!
HOW to EARN MILLION$
MOON MADE OF CHEESE
LIZARD PEOPLE
CLICK to SEE
FOLLOW THIS LINK
REAL FAKE
WORLD ENDING!
ELVIS LIVES
INVASION!
BAD GUYS
PIGS CAN FLY
NEW DISCOVERY

Maybe this stuff is true. Maybe it isn't. Before you decide, notice how it makes you *feel*. The world is full of stories, and many of them are true – they're carefully researched by scientists or journalists who are doing their best to get you the facts. But a lot of stories – sometimes called **FAKE NEWS** – are not true.

Sometimes they are trying to fool you; at other times they just want your attention. Either way, fake news stories often work by attracting your Brain Guard with something funny, or sad, or scary.

And your Brain Guard is very excitable. When you feel strong emotions, your Brain Guard is likely to make VERY DODGY DECISIONS. Your Brain Guard is also in a hurry, making very rapid first impressions. That can be useful, but it can also lead to BAD CHOICES. Instead, try to notice those strong emotions, slow down for a moment and be calm. That way your Brain Guard is much more likely to pay attention to logic and evidence. Sir Arthur's didn't. Yours can.

The Case Is Finally Solved

Finally, 65 years after Elsie and Frances took their first photographs of fairies, the *British Journal of Photography* published an amazing piece of detective work – a long series of articles which investigated every witness and examined every clue. There was no doubt, said the *British Journal of Photography*, that the pictures were faked. And it explained exactly how.

Each photograph included paper cut-outs of fairies, copied by Elsie from a picture book. One of them had been 'improved' by a photographic artist who'd been asked to enhance the image so that it would look good when it was displayed at a large size. Back then, there was no digital photo processing: artists would improve blurry patches by painting over the photograph with a fine brush. This artist had gone too far, adding lots of details from his imagination.

Another photograph combined two images, one of Frances and one of a cut-out of a fairy, making it look like it was hovering in front of Frances's gaze. Elsie was an expert at combining two photographs together. One of the jobs she often had to do at work was to combine a photograph of a soldier with a photograph of his family. It was sad work: the soldier would have been killed during the First World War and his family would have requested this combined photograph as it was the only way to show everyone together in one picture.

And just as the *British Journal of Photography* was explaining how the trick photographs had been made, they received a letter from an 82-year-old lady. Her name was . . . Elsie!

And Elsie had a confession to make . . .

TRUTH VILLAIN

Elsie Wright wasn't evil. In fact, I think she was rather wonderful. But she did play a trick and then lie about that trick for 65 years. Why? Elsie's letter to the *British Journal of Photography* explained that the whole thing had started as a joke, but that the girls had 'got ourselves into . . . the pickle' because Elsie's mother showed the photographs to other grown-ups – which is how it got to Sir Arthur Conan Doyle. Instead of being a family joke, the trick became too big: Sir Arthur was one of the most famous people in the country.

At first, Elsie was lying to protect her sister, and because she was proud of her skills as a photographer and an artist. In the end, she lied because it would have been cruel to reveal the truth. She couldn't confess without making Sir Arthur and her parents sad and embarrassed. So she kept quiet for most of her life, until she was old enough to be a great-grandmother herself. Elsie is a reminder that sometimes people lie out of kindness, not evil motives. But as Truth Detectives we still need to be alert and think clearly – unlike Sir Arthur.

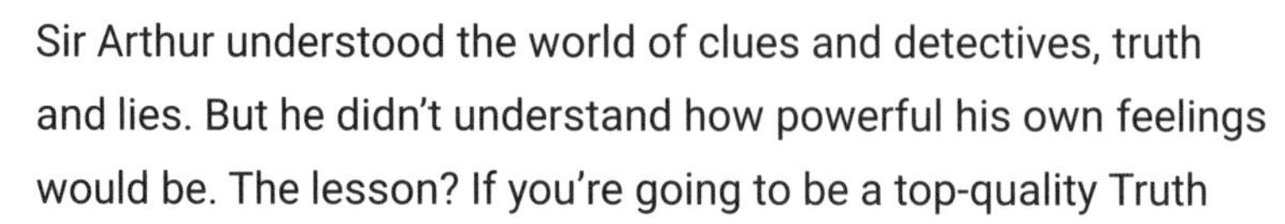

Sir Arthur understood the world of clues and detectives, truth and lies. But he didn't understand how powerful his own feelings would be. The lesson? If you're going to be a top-quality Truth Detective, you have to be able to notice your own feelings. You don't always have to control them – but you can make sure they don't control you.

TRICKS, TACTICS AND TOOLS

Let's think about what we've learned and make a plan of action for being better Truth Detectives:

1) Remember: your Brain Guard is making hasty decisions about which ideas you pay attention to and which you reject.

2) Follow Darth Vader's rule: search your feelings. When you see or hear a claim, how does it make you feel? What emotions does it stir in you? Your feelings may be getting in the way of clear thinking.

3) We're often under pressure to rush to judgements, and rushed judgements are often bad judgements. Slow down.

4) If somebody tells you they have photographed fairies at the bottom of the garden, you might want to think twice before you write an entire book about the photographs . . .

FIND YOUR MAGNIFYING GLASS – AND POINT IT IN THE RIGHT DIRECTION

Some things we can't see because they aren't there – such as fairies at the bottom of the garden. But there are lots of things we can only see if we look carefully and with the right equipment. In this chapter, we're going to talk about LENSES, from traditional glass lenses, as used by scientists and detectives, to lenses made out of numbers! So polish your magnifying glass and keep your telescope to hand as we try to see something that's all around us, but hard to pin down . . . rising prices.

The Case of the Pricey Pasta

If you talk to grown-ups for long enough (and it won't usually take long), they will start to tell you about how money used to be worth more in the old days. 'I remember when you could visit the funfair with tuppence, go on all the rides, buy a bag of candyfloss and still have change for the bus fare home,' they'll say. Yawn! But they have a point. Over time, everything seems to get more expensive.

For example, when I was young, the best toy in the world was the LEGO Galaxy Explorer. I wanted it for Christmas in 1981, and it was a really expensive toy: I know, because my father told me that he might not be able to afford it. (He was bluffing, maybe. Or maybe my grandparents helped. Either way, on Christmas morning, there it was, wrapped up under the Christmas tree.) The Galaxy Explorer was a huge LEGO set: a lunar landing pad, a control tower, four astronauts (two white, two red) and colossal spaceship with a loading bay for a space buggy.

Amazing! And the price? About £20 – it seemed a lot of money at the time, but when LEGO re-released the set, it was priced at £90, four or five times more. Why so much more money? It's partly that the new design is bigger and more complex. It's partly that they're hoping to sell it to nostalgic parents (like, um, me). But mostly? Mostly the LEGO is more expensive because EVERYTHING is more expensive.[4]

There's a word for this: **INFLATION**.[5] There's a number too.

---

[4] *If you are interested - and who isn't interested in LEGO? - websites such as Brickset and BrickEconomy provide amazing amounts of data on the price of different LEGO sets over time. But isn't it strange that we know so much about the price of oil, gold and LEGO but - as we'll soon see - not so much about the price of spaghetti?*

[5] *Which sounds fun, like blowing up a balloon or a bouncy castle. It isn't.*

In most countries, government **STATISTICIANS** regularly publish an estimate of how much prices have increased over the past year. (In the UK, these statisticians work for the **OFFICE FOR NATIONAL STATISTICS** or ONS.) If inflation is zero, prices haven't changed. If it's 100%, then prices have doubled. This is annoying – and if your pocket money isn't increasing but prices are, then over time you will be able to afford less and less. Being a Truth Detective won't protect you from inflation – but if you get savvy with the numbers you can see where it is happening, who is suffering the most and even how to protect some of the poorest people in our communities.

Not long ago, the official UK inflation number was about 5%, which was higher than people were used to. This level of inflation meant that prices had increased by about 5p for every £1 – a chocolate bar that cost £1 a year ago would now be £1.05. A £10 T-shirt would now be £10.50. A £1,000 computer would now be £1,050. And some people were angry, not just because things were getting more expensive, but because they were getting more expensive more quickly than usual.

Now, the intriguing thing about inflation of 5% is that although it's bigger than usual and big enough to cause problems, it's not *that* big. If you weren't paying attention, you might miss it. For example, that T-shirt. If you'd been saving up £10 to buy it, went to the shop and found it was now £10.50, you'd be FURIOUS. But if you hadn't been saving for it and you just went to the shop to see if there was something you wanted to buy, you might not notice. But one person who *was* keeping track of inflation was the food writer and campaigner Jack Monroe. For years, she had been carefully noting down the prices of food basics like baked beans and pasta and rice. Maybe computers and T-shirts were increasing in price by 5% – but her own experience was in cheap food, and she was discovering something very different.

Here are some of the clues she found:

In 2021, a can of baked beans had cost 22p; in 2022 it was 32p. That's inflation of nearly 50%.

In 2021, cheap pasta was 29p – but instead of increasing in price to 30p or 31p, it had more than doubled in price to 70p in 2022. That's inflation of more than 100%.

Even worse, a bag of rice had increased in price from 45p to 200p, or £2. That's an increase of more than 300%.

You might not notice a 5% increase, unless you were careful. But you'd certainly see a 300% increase!

The graphs on the next page use the data Jack Monroe collected to show how much prices were going up in just one year – much more than the official number of 5%.

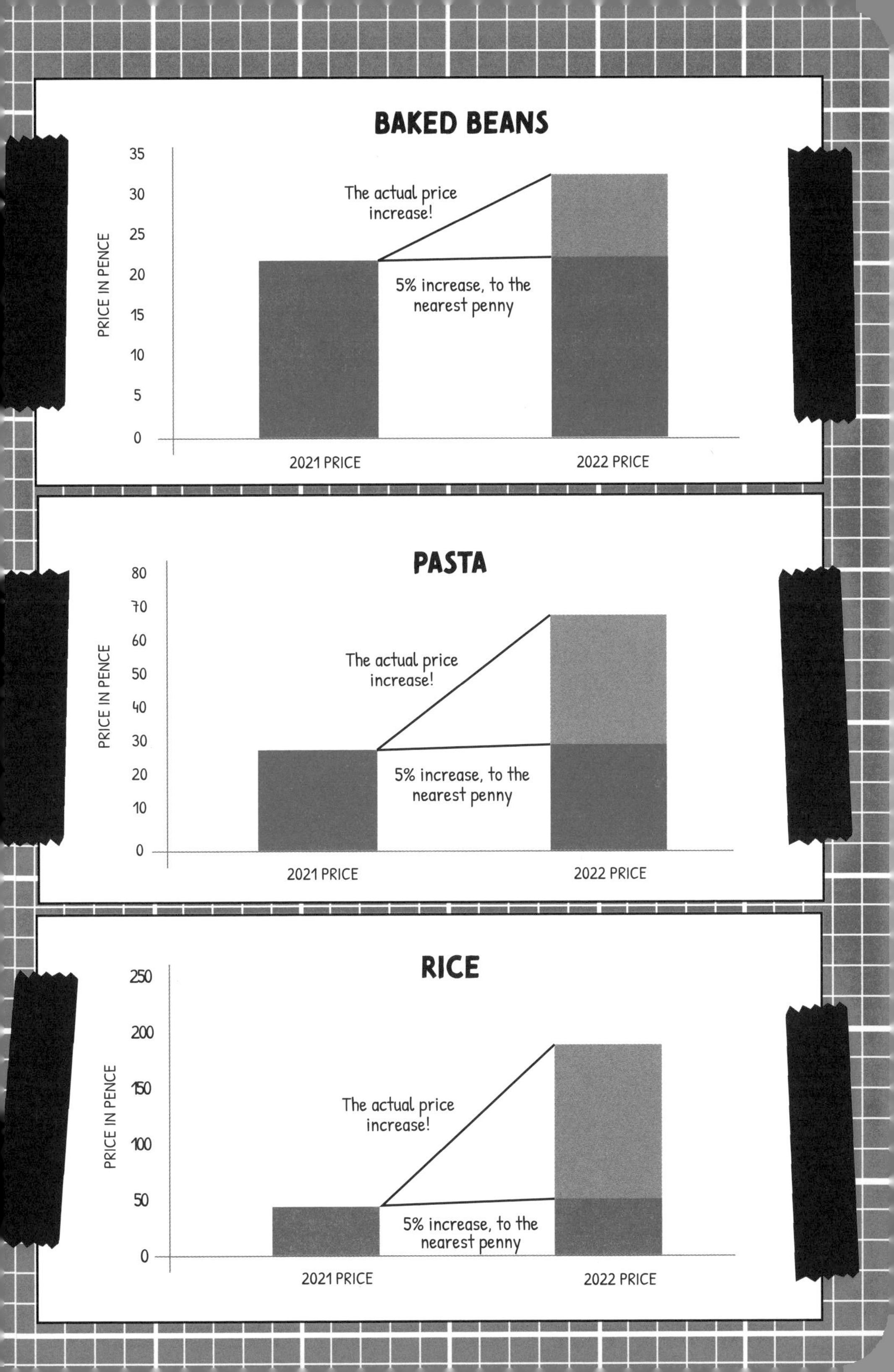
BAKED BEANS
PRICE IN PENCE
35
30
25
20
15
10
5
0
The actual price increase!
5% increase, to the nearest penny
2021 PRICE
2022 PRICE
PASTA
PRICE IN PENCE
80
70
60
50
40
30
20
10
0
The actual price increase!
5% increase, to the nearest penny
2021 PRICE
2022 PRICE
RICE
PRICE IN PENCE
250
200
150
100
50
0
The actual price increase!
5% increase, to the nearest penny
2021 PRICE
2022 PRICE

TRUTH DETECTIVE

When her son was a baby, Jack Monroe quit her job to look after him – and soon found herself out of money, even to buy food. Sometimes she would give him some food, like jam on toast, but didn't have enough for herself. He would ask why she wasn't eating. 'I'm not hungry,' she would tell him. But she was.

Jack started working out how to cook tasty food using the cheapest possible ingredients, and she posted her recipes on the internet. As more and more people started sharing her ideas, she began publishing books with her favourite recipes. But perhaps she is better known for her campaigns against poverty and her efforts to raise money for food banks.

As you can see from the charts, the price increases that Jack found when she went to her local supermarket were way bigger than you would expect if food prices were rising by 5%. But 5% was the official measure of inflation. So . . . what was happening? It was a curious case. To crack it, let's ask . . .

Where Is the Lens Pointing?

Magnifying glasses are very useful for any detective – using a simple lens on a handle, they take something tiny and make it look much bigger so that you can see it clearly. But the problem with a magnifying glass is that you can't point the lens everywhere at once. You can't make *everything* big and bold and clear. You have to choose.

I think that numbers can be a kind of lens – like a magnifying glass, a telescope or a microscope. They can show you something clearly that you wouldn't otherwise be able to see. When we gather and study lots of numbers that describe the world, we call them **STATISTICS.**

Statistics is the word both for all those numbers and for the science of studying the numbers.

Used properly, statistics can be as powerful a lens as any microscope or telescope.

And we can use the lens of statistics to understand inflation. As we've seen, just casually looking at prices – such as the price of a T-shirt – you might or might not notice inflation of about 5%. It's when you start collecting and comparing specific prices that you see what's really going on – that's what it means to turn the lens of statistics towards the problem of inflation. But where *exactly* should we point the lens?

Jack Monroe looked at the price of the cheapest foods at her local supermarket, and she found that they were increasing fast by huge amounts. But the UK's official statistics from the ONS showed only a small increase in prices. Why such a difference? Because they were pointing their lenses at different things.

Remember that inflation refers to rising prices. But rising prices of what? Let's say you only want to buy a Freddo (understandably) and the price of Freddos is increasing by 10% a year.[6] But broader inflation is just 5%. So what if your parents decide to increase your pocket money by just 5%?

'That's not fair!' you protest. 'I only want to buy chocolate frogs, so only the price of Freddos matters. You should increase my pocket money by 10%, not 5%.'[7]

What you think inflation is depends on what you want to buy. You're looking at the price of Freddos and Jack Monroe was looking at the price of the most basic food at her local supermarket. So what was the Office for National Statistics looking at?

Good question! The ONS looks at how the prices of

---

[6] *In case you don't know what a Freddo is, well - it was invented in Australia. It's a small bar of milk chocolate and it's, um, shaped like a funny cartoon frog. Because who doesn't want their chocolate to look like a frog, eh? What is more delicious than a frog?*

[7] *I'm not making this up, by the way. The price of Freddos has risen faster than general inflation. In 1999 a Freddo was usually 10p in the UK. In 2019 it was typically 30p. But if the price of Freddos had simply risen in line with the price of everything else, they would have cost only 15p in 2019. Freddoflation is higher than regular inflation.*

seven hundred different products change over time, checking the prices in lots of different shops. They call this list of seven hundred products the 'basket', because the idea is that you might go shopping and put them in your shopping basket. Although it contains things that you definitely shouldn't put in a shopping basket, like petrol or a mattress, and things you definitely *couldn't* put in a shopping basket, like a holiday on the beach or having a plumber unblock your toilet. The list of products changes over time, too – just take a look . . .

THE OFFICE FOR NATIONAL STATISTICS INFLATION 'BASKET'	
1956, A FEW YEARS AFTER THE SECOND WORLD WAR	**TODAY**
Prunes	Veggie burgers
Lard	Olive oil
Custard powder	Protein shakes
Jelly	Sweets
Knickers [8]	Underwear
Money order poundage [9]	Streaming subscription fee
Winceyette [10]	Replica football team shirt
Camera film and developing charge [11]	Inkjet printer cartridge
Toys: wooden building blocks	Toys: computer games console
. . . and other things	. . . and other things

[8] I'm pretty sure that we're talking about the same thing, but in 1956 statisticians were looking at the price tag on 'knickers', while now they look at the price tag on 'underwear'.

[9] Yes, I was confused too. I had to look it up. It's the cost of getting a special kind of document to send money along with a letter. These days we would send it electronically.

[10] I had to look this one up too. Apparently it's a type of soft cloth, the kind you would make pyjamas out of, if you were cutting and stitching your own pyjamas at home.

[11] Before you had cameras on phones, cameras would contain a roll of film. You'd take the film to a shop, and after a week or so you would go back and they would give you glossy card prints of your photographs. I can't believe I am having to explain this. I feel so old . . .

The ONS basket includes some basics, like milk, and some fancy stuff, like champagne. During the pandemic that started in 2020, the ONS added hand sanitiser, baggy lounge pants, pet toys and craft kits to the basket, to reflect the kind of things that people were buying. When the ONS said that inflation was 5%, that is the average rise it got when it looked at these and hundreds of other products.

But while the ONS pointed its magnifying glass at a lot of things, it didn't look at everything. For example, it looked at the price of champagne and holidays, and the most popular brands of pasta and rice – but not necessarily the very cheapest. Jack Monroe focused only on the cheapest food in her local supermarket. By pointing their lenses at different things, the ONS and Jack Monroe had found very different clues to the rate of inflation.

So who is right about inflation for people who have the least? The answer is: we don't know. We don't know because nobody has yet pointed their magnifying glass at a large range of the cheapest goods bought by the poorest families.

Can You Make Your Own Inflation Lens?

By now I hope we've learned at least three lessons.

First, numbers (or data, or STATISTICS) are like a lens: they can take something that's hard to see and make it clear.

BUT . . . Second, the lens can't show you everything. You might point it at one clue, someone else might look at a different clue. And you'd learn different things.

Third, IT MATTERS where you point the lens. If you want to buy chocolate, but your parents don't properly increase your pocket money, you're going to be able to buy less chocolate. This matters for grown-ups too. If their income changes in line with the official inflation number (as it often does) but the official inflation number is looking at posh food and holidays, while they want to buy cheap pasta and baked beans, they're going to struggle.

Jack Monroe decided the best way to fix the problem was to get help – more volunteers, all collecting information about the price of basic goods such as the cheapest bread and pasta, frozen vegetables and canned food, and hygiene products like shampoo and toothpaste. She wants to get a BIGGER, BETTER LENS. (She's called it the Vimes Boots Index, after a character in a book by Terry Pratchett called Captain Vimes.)

Captain Vimes

Captain Vimes complained that a rich person could afford high-quality boots that would last and last. A poor person didn't have enough money in their purse to do that, so they could only afford boots that would soon wear out. Then they would have to buy a replacement, and another replacement, and another replacement. At the end of ten years, the rich person would still have their high-quality boots. The poor person would have had to buy cheap boots every winter. In total they would have spent twice as much as the rich person – and would still have wet feet.

The Vimes 'Boots' theory is that rich people end up paying less for all kinds of things. Do you think it's true?

My guess is that it's true for some things and not true for others. But if we had good DATA – well, we wouldn't need to guess, would we?

If you were making your own inflation basket, what would you put in it? Sherlock Holmes, perhaps the most famous detective of all, is often portrayed wearing a strange hat called a 'deerstalker'. He smoked too much, played the violin, carried a pistol and used a microscope to examine clues – so this is what you might find in his basket:

I lead a less glamorous life, although I use a laptop a lot (for both writing and calculations) and play a lot of games with dice. When I'm not reading or writing, I am fond of fancy sandwiches and Japanese noodles. And I don't smoke, which is perhaps the only way in which I am smarter than Sherlock Holmes. So this is what my basket would look like:

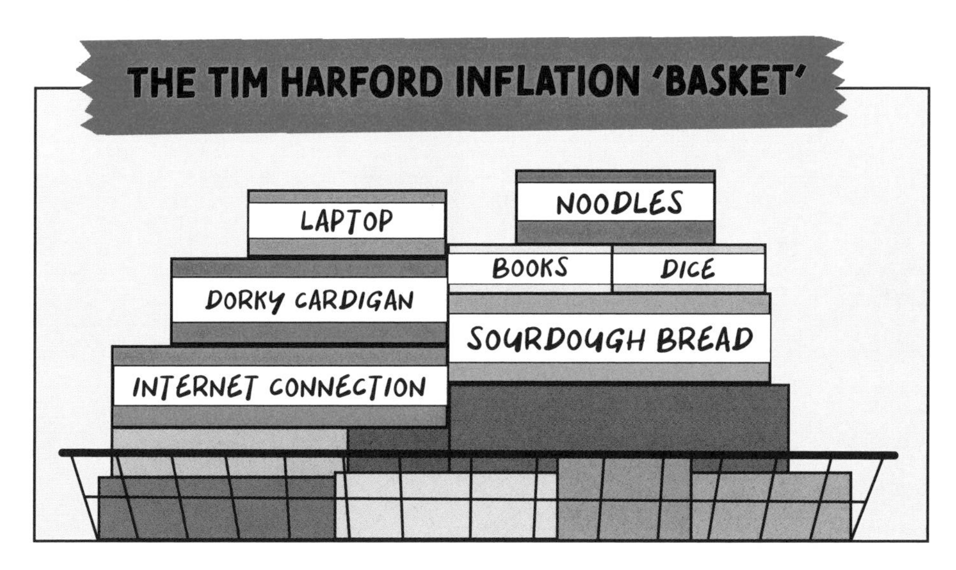

What would be in *your* inflation basket? Grab yourself a piece of paper or a notebook and write down the things you'd be most happy to see get cheaper – and that you'd be most upset about if they got more expensive.

It isn't easy to figure out how prices are changing. The Office for National Statistics has decided that in the future, it's going to try to do better than just look at the prices of seven hundred products. Instead, it will use electronic data from the scanners at checkouts to capture the price of everything. So the inflation lens is getting bigger and better! And the better the magnifying glass, the easier it is to see clearly something important about how life is changing – something that would otherwise be impossible to see.

Jack Monroe is trying to get a bigger, better magnifying glass. And the Office for National Statistics is trying to do the same thing. Although they don't agree about everything, they *do* agree that this matters. Numbers are like a lens: they help us see more clearly.

But the strange thing is – not *everyone* wants to look through a good lens, as we're about to learn.

Refusing to Look Through the Telescope

Galileo was a mathematician and scientist born in 1564 near Pisa, in Italy. People tell lots of stories about Galileo – for example, that he settled an old argument by dropping a heavy ball and a light ball from the top of the famous leaning tower of Pisa.[8] Ancient thinkers believed that the heavy ball would fall faster, but they were wrong: the two balls hit the ground at the same time.

The details of that story probably aren't right (other scientists did the experiment before Galileo was born), but the story lasts because it's cool, and because it shows us something important about Galileo's character: if you want to understand the world, don't just think – *look*.

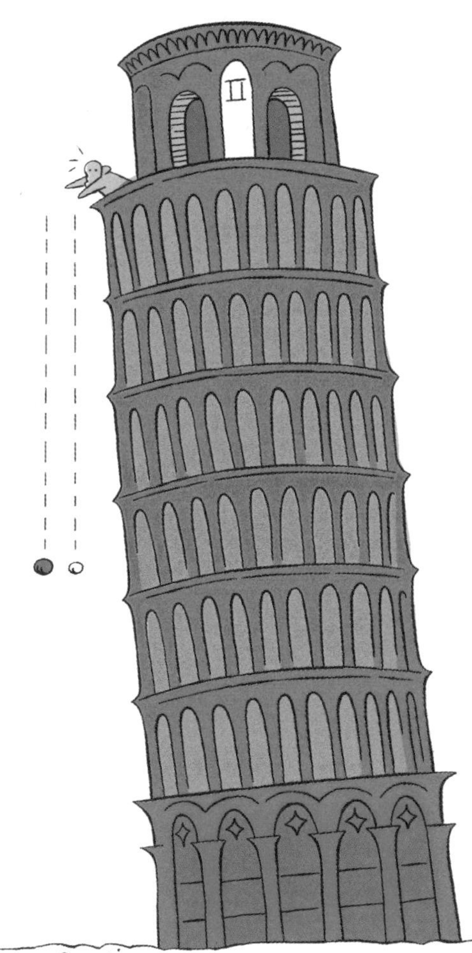

Another famous story about Galileo is the time he disagreed with another scientist about the moon. His critic argued that the moon, the sun and other objects up in the sky were all perfect spheres. Galileo looked through his telescope and could see

[8] *If you are now planning to climb up a very wonky tower and drop a cannonball from the top, please stop.*

mountains and valleys on the moon. It wasn't a perfect sphere – it was a big old crinkly hunk of rock. 'Just take a look for yourself!' said Galileo. His critic refused. Big mistake. Again: *look*.

People argue today about which parts of that story are true. Did people really refuse to look through Galileo's telescope? I think they probably did refuse, because I keep seeing the same refusal all around me today.

THE BRAIN GUARDS ARE BACK

One of the best lenses we have today is statistical: look at the right numbers, and you'll get the right clues. But lots of people have decided – or perhaps their Brain Guards have decided – that they don't want to look at the numbers. Partly because they might be afraid that the numbers would be too confusing or complicated. But often, like Galileo's critics, they don't want to look because they are afraid that what they see could prove them wrong. Nowhere is that more true than when it comes to the invisible crisis we call climate change . . .

Seeing Climate Change by Using Statistics

Sunshine or rain, snow or mist, it's easy to see the weather. But can you see the climate? For more than two thousand years, European scientists followed the ancient Greek philosopher Aristotle in their view of what the climate was. It's simple, said Aristotle: at the poles, it's cold. Near the equator, it's hot. Between the equator and each pole is a middling zone, where the climate is pleasant.

But actually, it's not so simple. The climate does change, both for natural reasons and because we humans have been polluting the atmosphere. But the climate changes very slowly, and random changes in the weather tend to obscure climate change. One month might be unusually cold, another unusually hot. People can't see climate change just by looking around – the weather gets in the way!

Instead, we need to collect statistics. As before, statistics are the lens we use to look for tiny clues. All around the world, weather detectives are gathering measurements of the weather. Now, there are thousands of weather stations all over the surface of the world, plus instruments attached to the front of aircraft, floating on buoys or attached to ships in the ocean, and of course weather satellites orbiting the world, always watching. The weather detectives are on the case!

But to see the patterns amidst all these different measurements, we need the science of statistics. Statistics is the lens that helps us organise lots and lots of numbers – and see something as subtle and slow moving as climate change. Without it, all we could do is talk about the weather. Some people don't want to admit that the data shows the climate is changing: their Brain Guards have taken over and would rather not think about the problem, or how they might have to change their own lives to respond. But most people now understand that the climate is changing and that the change is dangerous – and also, more hopefully, people understand the kind of changes they now need to fight for.

Is inflation higher for people without much money? How fast is the climate changing? The world is full of important questions that we can't answer without getting a really good, clear view through the lens of statistics.

If you have a question you want answered, look for evidence in the form of numbers. Carefully collected numbers can show us truths we can't see by just looking around.

) Sometimes the numbers aren't available. If so, make some noise like Jack Monroe! It takes effort to gather data, whether it's the price of cheap pasta or the temperature of the Indian Ocean over time. Speak up about what matters to help make sure that effort is focused in the right place.

3) Remember Galileo's telescope. Sometimes people won't look at the evidence because they're afraid it will be confusing – or will prove them wrong. Don't be one of those people. Be willing to look.

4) Always carry some spare Freddos. You never know when you might need them – and apparently they're more valuable every day . . .

KNOW WHEN TO PUT THE LENS DOWN

Looking through the Lens of Statistics and Looking with Your Own Eyes

The last chapter was all about lenses, and numbers provide a wonderful lens to look at the world. But no detective should rely on the same tool every time. You wouldn't get very far interviewing witnesses, or in a daring car chase to catch the villains, if you were squinting through a magnifying glass the whole time. Sometimes you need to put aside the magnifying glass and the telescope, and look around with your own eyes. So when is it better to trust your own experience? And how can we avoid our all-too-emotional Brain Guard leaping to the wrong conclusions?

One hint comes from Muhammad Yunus. Muhammad was used to looking at the world through the lens of statistics. Born in Bangladesh, he studied economics in the United States of America, where he learned all about the power of gathering and analysing the numbers.

But when he returned to Bangladesh, he found that the statistics that were available didn't do a good job of describing the lives of the poorest people. There wasn't enough information to figure out how desperate they really were, and certainly not enough to find a solution to their poverty. And so he decided he needed to go out of the university classroom to meet the poor women who worked in nearby villages. These women were skilled basket-weavers, but they often had to borrow money to cover their costs, and the moneylenders charged so much that the women had almost nothing left for themselves.

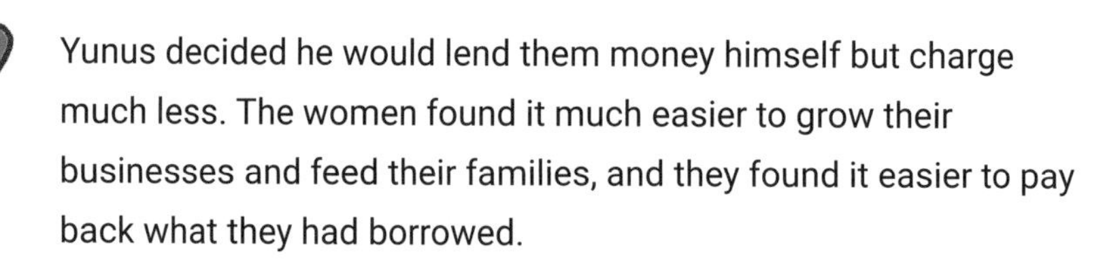

Yunus decided he would lend them money himself but charge much less. The women found it much easier to grow their businesses and feed their families, and they found it easier to pay back what they had borrowed.

TRUTH DETECTIVE

Muhammad Yunus became known as the 'Banker to the Poor' after he set up the Grameen Bank in 1983. Grameen Bank made the same tiny loans to small businesses, at the same low prices that Yunus himself had given to the basket-weavers.

MUHAMMAD YUNUS

Grameen Bank became famous around the world, and this idea of 'microfinance' was copied in many countries. Muhammad Yunus and Grameen Bank shared the Nobel Peace Prize in 2006 for their work reducing poverty.

Yunus advocated what he sometimes called 'the worm's eye view'. Instead of the 'bird's eye view', where you fly high and see everything from a great distance, try moving slowly, looking carefully and taking the time to think about what you see. That's the 'worm's eye view'.

Although looking at life through a statistical lens is very powerful, sometimes a Truth Detective needs to put the lens to one side and just look around, like Muhammad Yunus did.

Statistics give us the big picture, showing us things like climate change or inflation that we can only understand when we can analyse the patterns in a lot of information. But our personal experience shows us something else. Think about Jack Monroe's realisation that there might be a problem with the price of cheap pasta. It didn't come from looking at columns and columns of numbers. It came from visiting the local shop and thinking, 'Hm – that doesn't seem right. That's more expensive than I remember.' Personal experience matters.

Talking about a rise in average global temperatures is one thing, but you truly understand the power of changing weather patterns when your home is flooded. Inflation can only be properly measured through lots of numbers, but you feel it when you've grown out of your shoes and your parents can't afford a new pair. To really understand the world, you need statistics (the telescope and the magnifying glass). But you also need your own experience: to see the world not through a spreadsheet, but as a human.

TRUTH DETECTIVE

One of the Truth Detectives I most admire is Hans Rosling. Hans trained as a statistician but also as a doctor, and he began his working life meeting people all over the world who were sick and who had no money. One of his early cases was a mysterious outbreak of a disease called konzo, in Mozambique, Africa. Nobody knew what was causing the illness – some people even suspected that it might be a deliberate attack with chemical weapons.

Hans and his colleagues eventually worked out that the cause was a kind of poisonous vegetable that needed to be very carefully prepared to make it safe. Because there was a famine, some people had become so hungry they ate the vegetable too soon.

This was one of many adventures Hans had in his life, combining the human spirit with the use of statistics to understand and solve people's problems.

Hans became one of the great communicators – using statistics to solve problems, but never forgetting the humans behind them.

Although Hans became the most famous statistician in the world, he once wrote that 'Numbers will never tell the full story of what life on Earth is all about.' Numbers are essential, but we need to look with our own eyes too.

A few years ago, I visited China with my family. I already had a statistical view: I knew that China was moving fast from being very poor, through being middle-income, towards being rich.

But it was only when I personally visited that I got to feel what that was like. We travelled by train across southern China, seeing skyscrapers that make the famous Empire State Building in New York seem small, and passing tower block after tower block after tower block, stretching away into the distance. So many people. So much concrete. I was looking at an amazing escape from poverty for the Chinese, but I was wondering: how could the planet possibly survive such dramatic growth, on top of all the economic growth already seen in Western countries?

There was nothing about this scene that I didn't already know from the numbers. But seeing it up close was different. I went from knowing something from a distance to feeling it and understanding it.

When the Personal View Is Wrong

We need to be careful that our personal viewpoint doesn't lead us astray. When you get too close to something, you can easily miss the fact that life may look very different elsewhere. Think about Jack Monroe's investigation into cheap pasta. She found prices rising incredibly fast in her local supermarket. But what if those prices weren't rising fast elsewhere? In fact, some experts reckoned that one particular supermarket chain had decided to get rid of the cheapest products in some of its stores. If, like Jack, you shopped for cheap pasta in one of those stores, things would look really bad. But if you were shopping in a different place, nothing would change. That's why it was important for Jack to start her Vimes Boots Index, rather than just looking at her own shopping basket.

It's easy to make a similar mistake with what's popular – music, hobbies or books. You and your friends might love a particular game, or band, or author – and it's easy to think that the whole world thinks the same. It can be strange to talk to someone a little older or younger, from a different country or even from a different school, and discover that their interests are totally different. Your own experience is a valuable window on to the world, letting you understand something in rich, vivid detail. But never forget that other people may see the world very differently.

The Problem with Getting Your Personal View from the News

When we watch the TV news, or follow news stories online or on social media, we often see very vivid videos and pictures. In fact, these news images are so vivid that we often feel like we have personally experienced them. You will see tanks exploding, buildings collapsing, planes crashing, ships sinking and scary photographs of convicted or suspected criminals.

But the good news is that although these frightening things do happen, they are not likely to happen near you. Most people will never see a plane crashing or a ship sinking. Even people who live in a war zone do not often see tanks exploding, and thankfully most people do not live in a war zone. But because of TV and internet news, you can be living somewhere very safe and still see these things happening every day, right in front of you on the screen.

When researchers ask people questions about their view of the world, people often think the world is more dangerous than it really is. The lens of statistics can show us how often there are crimes, wars or even illnesses such as diabetes. Statistics show us that crime has been falling in most countries – but most people think it is rising. We think that deaths from terrorist attacks have increased, but actually they have fallen.

We are often wrong about the world because we are looking at the news, and the news always shows us what is surprising and interesting – and often, what is frightening.

Movies, books and TV shows can also confuse us. Sometimes it's easy to see that an imaginary story is just an imaginary story. For example, aliens, giant gorillas and supervillains seem to spend a lot of time attacking us in the movies, and thankfully this has yet to happen in reality.[9] But often a made-up story can seem very real.

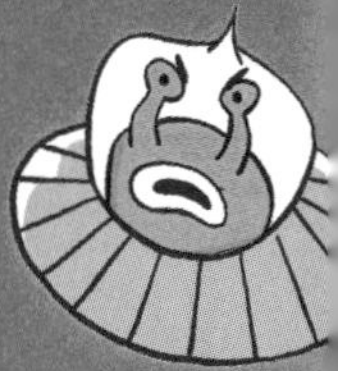

For example, there are lots of TV detective shows about murders. Murders do happen in the real world but in most places they are rare. (Thank goodness.) Yet on a TV detective show, murders have to happen a lot, otherwise there wouldn't be a new story each week. Chief Inspector Barnaby, the central character of the TV show *Midsomer Murders*, has to deal with a murder rate nearly 280 times higher than the true murder rate in England and Wales.

---

9 But if it ever does, we all know which city is going to be attacked, don't we? New York, every time.

Much the same is true of the *Inspector Morse* TV show, which is set in my home town of Oxford. (If it was really as dangerous as the TV show suggests, I would be scared to walk out of my front door.)

In reality, very few places on the planet have a murder rate comparable to these terrifying TV towns.[10] Places like London or New York, which often seem scary and dangerous on TV, aren't anywhere close to being as dangerous as Midsomer.

Again: the statistics tell you that murder is rare. Your own personal experience (I hope) also tells you that murder is rare. But the TV reshapes your personal feelings to tell a different story.

Dollar Street

You make the smartest decisions when you're able to use the statistical magnifying glass and telescope as well as looking around and using your personal experience. But doing both at the same time is not so easy! Trying to focus one eye on something up close and the other eye on something else on the horizon is going to give you headaches. But, like patting your head and rubbing your tummy at the same time, it's something you can learn to do with practice. And it's worth it!

For example: good encyclopaedia and reference books are full of vivid pictures and surprising information. They will show you the

[10] Probably not where you live, don't worry.

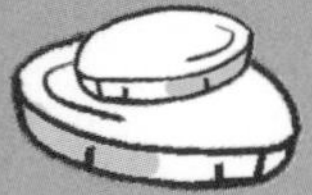

inside of a human body, zoom in to the size of a speck of dust or zoom out to show you the entire solar system, and give you cutaway diagrams of a medieval castle or a moon rocket. But amid all these wonders, you'll get careful, accurate information about the facts and the data. These are good books for any Truth Detective to have or to look for in a library.

Other tools are right at our fingertips – for example, the nifty Dollar Street website. Ask your parent or caregiver to help you go online and look at it. Dollar Street tries to give people an insight into how families live in different places. Dollar Street researchers visited the homes of volunteer families all over the world. They took photographs and videos of everything, and asked the families about their lives, their problems and their dreams. Now anyone who can go online can see what life is like for the Kabura family in Burundi, who make about $29 a month – a dollar a day – and live in a mud hut. Someday soon they hope to buy a bed. You can see how they cook (a fire on the bare earth floor) or brush their teeth (one toothbrush to share) and what their toilet is like (outside, with wooden boards over a hole in the ground). The children's favourite toy is some stuffing inside cloth, vaguely in the shape of an animal (maybe a dog?).

KABURA FAMILY

HANSEN REFSING FAMILY

Think about your own life.

- **Do you have a toilet?**
- **Does it have a flush and a door you can close so you can use the toilet in private?**
- **What about the kitchen – do your family cook with an open fire, electricity or gas?**
- **What are your favourite toys? (Maybe you also love a floppy stuffed thing more than anything else.)**

And as you think about your home, you can click to visit other families – for example, the Li family from China, who earn $731 a month. Or the Hansen Refsing family, who live in Denmark and are lucky enough to have more than $5,000 a month. Or more than 250 other families all over the world.

But Dollar Street doesn't just *show* photographs: all the photographs are comparable. You can see all the toilets compared, or all the toothbrushes, or all the toys. And you can see how those things vary – or don't – between rich and poor homes. For example, the most loved toy in the Hansen Refsing family home is a snuggly floppy teddy bear. In some ways it's totally different to what the Kabura children play with; in other ways it's just the same: a soft stuffed animal to cuddle.

This is the kind of evidence that any Truth Detective should examine! On Dollar Street you can get up close, looking at a toothbrush or a toilet. Or you can zoom out to look at the big picture, getting a sense of how people's lives are the same, or different, depending on where they live – and how much money they have. It's the magnifying glass, the telescope and the human gaze all in the same place. That's rare – and the kind of tool that a Truth Detective will treasure.

TRUTH DETECTIVE

Anna Rosling Rönnlund is the creator of Dollar Street. She is a brilliant data communicator – like her husband's father Hans Rosling, who we met earlier in this chapter. Anna designed software to help Hans give famous talks about how people really live all around the world: her software took numbers and turned them into animated bubbles that brought the big picture to life. For a few years she worked at Google on the same graph-drawing software. Now she is vice president of the Gapminder Foundation, which aims to help people use numbers to understand the world around them.

A good Truth Detective needs to feel comfortable using the magnifying glass and the telescope of statistics – but also be able to put down those lenses and just look around. Personal experience teaches us a lot – but it can also deceive us if our experience (or what we see on the news) is different from what other people are seeing. It can be hard to get the right balance, but it's important to try.

CLASSIFIED

TRICKS, TACTICS AND TOOLS

1) Look around and notice the world. Your personal experience is important and gives you useful clues about how the world works.

2) BUT don't rely only on that experience. What's true for you may be very different for other people, and what you see on the news is often much scarier than most people's everyday lives.

3) Use the statistical magnifying glass to help you see things close up, or the statistical telescope to scan the horizon and see the big picture – but don't hesitate to put the lens aside and combine data with your ordinary experience. Tools such as Dollar Street can help give you both perspectives.

4) Also, did you know you can use a magnifying glass to make one eye look super huge and creepy? Worth thinking about.

SEEK THE TRUTH WITH STATISTICS

I'm the oldest of four children, and when my little sisters were born, I'd ask my mum: where did these babies come from? I think she felt I was a little too young to know the details, so she told me that the babies had been brought by the stork.

It's an old story: storks deliver babies, carrying them in their beaks in big white fluffy blankets. But here's something that may surprise you: the numbers show that storks DO deliver babies. The countries with the most storks are also the countries with the most babies. And the countries with the most babies are also the countries with the most storks! That seems . . . odd. What's going on?

The Correlation Clue

This kind of pattern is called a **correlation** – when one thing often goes hand in hand with another. A correlation is sometimes

AN IMPORTANT CLUE – something might be going on. Then again, it might not be. Sometimes a correlation is pure chance – what we call a red herring.[11]

For example – did you know that there is a strange relationship between venomous spiders and spelling tests? It's true. In the US there is a strong correlation between the number of people in the US killed by venomous spiders and the number of letters in the final word in a famous spelling competition. For a couple of years the winning words were quite short (9 letters, 8 letters) and not many people were killed by spiders (6 deaths, 5 deaths). Then the words got longer (12 letters, 11 letters) and the spiders got busier (10 deaths, 8 deaths). The year with the longest word (13 letters) was also the worst year for spiders (14 deaths). Then, thankfully, both the spider deaths and the word lengths fell (7 letters, 5 deaths).

So – what could have caused this correlation? Are the spiders trying to win spelling competitions and taking out their opponents one bite at a time? Of course not. It's a fluke – one of those red herrings. And if you're astonished that there's such a strong relationship between spider deaths and spelling, don't be: there are so many things happening in the world that if you look hard enough, you're bound to find some coincidences.

---

[11] *A 'red herring' has come to mean a distraction from the truth. A red herring is a particularly stinky kind of smoked fish. REALLY STINKY. The idea is that if you want to escape from a bloodhound or another tracker dog, you can distract them from your scent with the red herring. Did I mention that it is VERY STINKY? By the way, this does not work. The dog will find the stinky fish, eat the stinky fish and then pick up your scent again. As a Truth Detective, you are not obliged to eat stinky fish but you do need to be careful to stay on the real trail and not be distracted.*

NUMBER OF LETTERS IN WINNING WORDS OF SCRIPPS NATIONAL SPELLING BEE
correlates with
NUMBER OF PEOPLE KILLED BY VENOMOUS SPIDERS

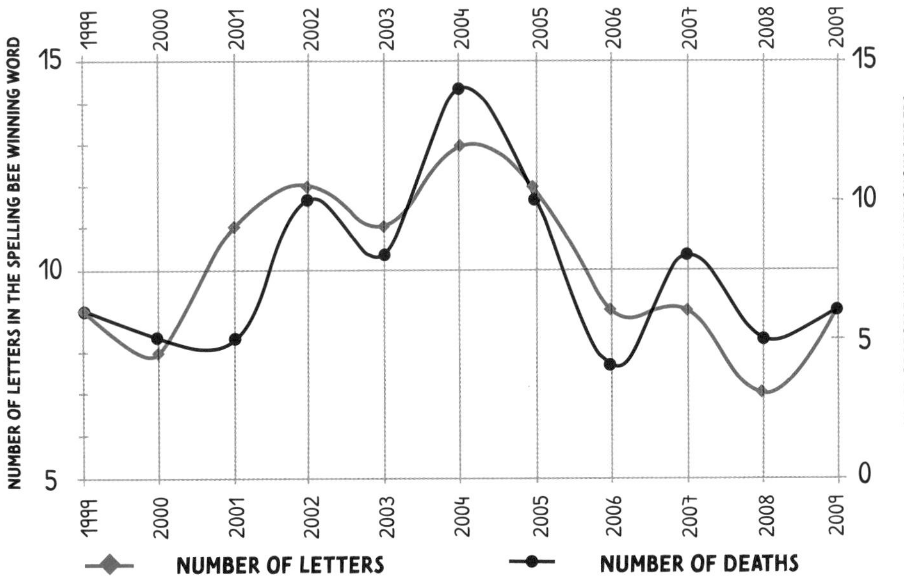

This graph is an adaptation of the original from Tyler Vigen's Spurious Correlations project: https://tylervigen.com/view_correlation?id=2941.

But correlations can *still* be red herrings even when they aren't flukes. For example, children with bigger shoes score better on maths tests. Should we try to improve everyone's test scores by giving them larger shoes? No. The correlation is real but big shoes don't cause high maths scores. Instead, fifteen-year-olds usually have bigger feet (and bigger shoes) than ten-year-olds, and ten-year-olds have bigger feet (and bigger shoes) than five-year-olds. And of course older children will usually do better at maths, too.

This is called a **CAUSAL FORK** (no, you can't eat spaghetti with a causal fork).

Here, there really is something going on behind the relationship between shoe size and maths test scores – but you can't just assume that big shoes cause test scores to rise (or that high test scores cause shoes to get bigger). A good Truth Detective treats the correlation clue as a signal to look deeper.

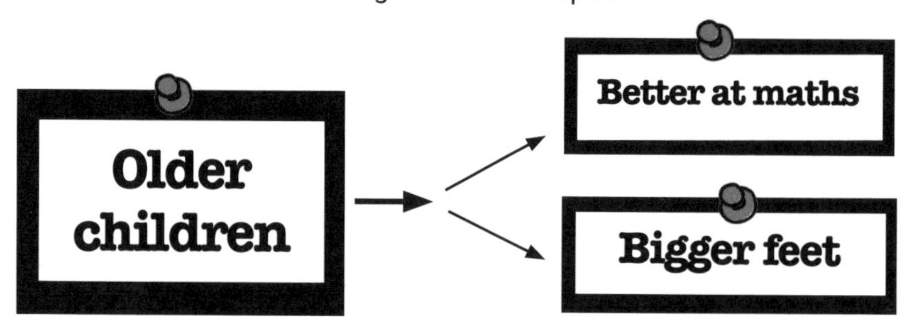

So what's happening with the storks and the babies? Might it be another causal fork? Think about a large country like Poland or Turkey: lots of babies, lots of storks. Now think of a tiny place like Monaco or Luxembourg: not many babies, not many storks.[12] When you see that places with lots of babies also have lots of storks, what you're really seeing is that large countries have lots of room for both.

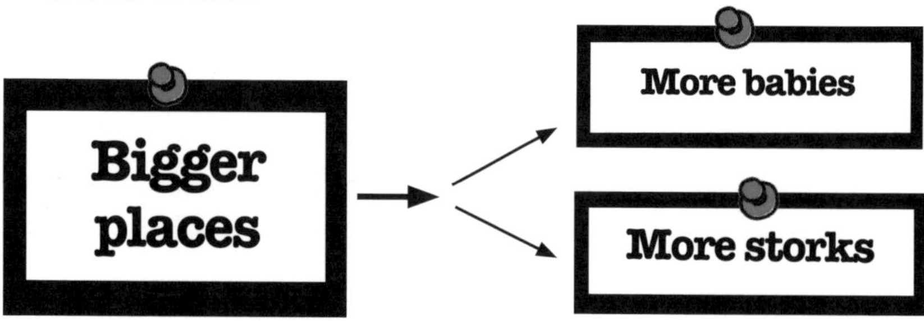

[12] Monaco and Luxembourg are both countries, but Luxembourg has the same population as a medium-sized city, while the population of Monaco is the same as a small town.

Storks, Babies and the Strange Case of the Deaths from Lung Cancer

One of the most famous books ever written about statistics is *How to Lie with Statistics* by Darrell Huff. Huff filled his book with fun examples of all the ways in which statistics could deceive us – including the example of the correlation between storks and babies. I loved reading the book when I was young. It was one of the reasons I became so interested in statistics and how they can mislead us.

But there was one important thing missing from Huff's book: he didn't include many examples of statistics being used to figure out the *truth*. That turns out to be a big problem – because when statistics are used to figure out the truth, the results can be *life-saving*.

In the 1950s, just as *How to Lie with Statistics* was being published, doctors and scientists were puzzling over a strange mystery. An unusual but very dangerous illness, lung cancer, was becoming much more common over time. Over the course of just fifteen years, deaths from lung cancer in the UK had increased six times over – a huge increase. But what was causing this deadly rise?

Two British scientists, Richard Doll and Austin Bradford Hill, decided to investigate. First they interviewed lots of hospital patients, with and without cancer, about where they lived and worked, what they ate and how much they exercised – and also whether they smoked. The results of this initial work suggested a clue: perhaps smoking cigarettes was contributing to lung cancer. (Like many people at the time, Doll and Hill were smokers. Richard Doll later said, 'I did not expect to find smoking was a major problem.' But as the evidence from their research began to build up, both of them gave up smoking.)

To follow up, Doll and Hill wrote to nearly sixty thousand doctors about their health and their smoking habits. It soon became very clear: people who smoked were much more likely to develop lung cancer – not two or three times more likely, but sixteen times more likely.

This was a vitally important discovery, because in the 1950s a huge number of people smoked cigarettes. Even a small danger could kill a lot of people – and it turns out that this danger wasn't small. Other scientists

were finding similar clues around the same time, and gradually we came to realise that smoking was a very dangerous habit. But the wonderful thing is that by discovering the danger, scientists could warn people not to start smoking – or to stop smoking as soon as they could.

It took time for the message to get out, and it also took time for people to quit, because smoking is very addictive. I am old enough to remember when restaurants, aeroplanes and even schools had areas set aside for smoking. And people who are older than me remember when *everywhere* was a smoking area – you could even smoke inside hospitals. But gradually people realised the danger and protected themselves by avoiding cigarettes. Millions and millions of lives have been saved as a result.

It's an important reminder that while statistics can be used by evil masterminds to trick us, they can also be used by scientists, researchers and Truth Detectives to show us the truth. We can't do what Darrell Huff did and simply focus only on the lies. We have to look for the truth as well – and the numbers can help us. Numbers, remember, can show us invisible things. The link between cigarettes and cancer was one of those invisible things.

TRUTH DETECTIVE

SIR AUSTIN BRADFORD HILL

Sir Austin 'Tony' Bradford Hill was a pilot in the First World War, but developed a disease called tuberculosis, which put him in hospital for two years and nearly killed him. After recovering, he felt he was too old to train as a doctor, so instead became an economist and later a statistician.

Some doctors did not like being sent a questionnaire asking them about their smoking habits. One of them met Hill at a party. 'You're the chap who wants us all to stop smoking,' he said.

'Not at all,' said Hill. 'I'm interested, if you go on smoking, to see how you die . . . choose for yourself, stop or go on. It's a matter of indifference to me. I shall score up your death anyway.'

Not a diplomat – but a brilliant Truth Detective whose work with Richard Doll helped save many millions of lives.

Austin Bradford Hill is also famous for running the first high-quality experiment to test the effectiveness of a medicine. He showed that an antibiotic could cure tuberculosis, the disease that had nearly killed him as a young man. Sweet statistical revenge!

How to Lie with *How to Lie with Statistics*

When politicians in the United States were debating whether to put health warnings on packets of cigarettes, an expert came to share his opinion about the question. Of course there was a correlation between cigarettes and lung cancer, he agreed. But there was also a correlation between storks and babies.

Surely the two cases were different? 'The two seem to me the same,' replied the expert.

It was . . . **DARRELL HUFF!**

(And he was not really an expert in anything that mattered, such as cancer or medical statistics – he was just a writer who wrote a fun book about numbers.) But the tobacco companies used people like Huff to confuse ordinary citizens about cigarettes. So many different opinions! People's Brain Guards were totally confused – and that was often an excuse for people who didn't want to stop smoking.

TRUTH VILLAIN

Darrell Huff's book *How to Lie with Statistics* is full of fun ideas and wise advice. It makes me so sad that Huff ended up accepting money from the cigarette industry to cast doubt on the idea that cigarettes were dangerous. The cigarette companies were worried because scientific evidence suggested that cigarettes were deadly. They wanted someone who could attack that scientific evidence, and Huff was the perfect person. Huff was famous for showing all the ways in which statistics fool us. He found it easy to argue that the statistics were fooling us yet again.

What was Huff thinking? I'm sure he must have been influenced by the money. But perhaps he had also spent so long thinking about statistical lies that he had forgotten that statistics could also tell us the truth.

Cigarettes really do cause cancer and other serious diseases, and slowly people came to accept that fact. But the strategy of casting doubt is very common. You might have noticed that lots of people don't believe climate change is happening or aren't sure either way, despite the fact that most climate scientists believe it is. **WHY IS THIS?**

It might be because oil and coal companies have tried the same tactic as the cigarette companies: attack the scientific research and encourage people to doubt everything. Just as cigarette companies wanted people to keep smoking the cigarettes they made, oil and coal companies want people to keep burning the fossil fuels they sell.

Some people have made similar arguments to claim that COVID-19 isn't real either. After all, you can't see climate change and you can't see a COVID-19 pandemic – all you can see are numbers. And as Darrell Huff taught us, numbers can be used to lie.

A real detective has to deal with people accused of crimes. They can't just assume all the accused people are guilty, and they can't assume they're all innocent either. The job of a detective is to collect evidence to help figure out the truth.

It's the same for a Truth Detective. When you see an eye-catching statistical claim, don't just assume it's true. It might be nonsense, like the link between storks and babies.

But don't assume it's false either. It might be a vital, life-saving fact, like the link between cigarettes and cancer. Your job as a Truth Detective isn't to believe everything, but it isn't to disbelieve everything either. It's to work out the difference between truth and lies. Are the kids with big shoes really smarter? Or are they just older? Does eating ice cream cause sunshine, or is it the other way around? So get out your cork noticeboard, sticky notes and string – and let's start making sense of the clues around us. To do that, we're going to need some

TRUTH DETECTIVE SKILLS.

KEEP READING . . .

TRICKS, TACTICS AND TOOLS

1) From storks and babies to smoking and lung cancer, lots of things seem to vary together – meaning they are *correlated.* Some correlations are vital clues; others are red herrings. Be careful to figure out which is which.

2) Evil masterminds (in the cigarette industry and elsewhere) have often tried to distract Truth Detectives from the evidence. Some statistical evidence is misleading, they say. True. But not ALL statistical evidence is misleading. Don't be diverted!

3) It's not smart to believe everything you read. But it's not smart to *disbelieve* everything, either. Darrell Huff looked for reasons to disbelieve; Doll and Bradford Hill looked for the truth. In the end, it was Doll and Bradford Hill who saved millions upon millions of lives.

4) If you're entering a spelling contest, watch out for venomous spiders. I know I said it was a fluke – but I wonder. Those spiders can be pretty sneaky.

SECTION TWO

FAKE

EWS

THE SKILLS OF A TRUTH DETECTIVE

OBSERVE THE LABEL

The famous detective Sherlock Holmes (in the story 'A Scandal in Bohemia') once explained to his friend Dr Watson:

I'm not suggesting that you should spend your time counting and memorising the number of steps on the staircases you encounter. But a good Truth Detective needs to be observant, and the most obvious thing to observe, which others miss, is the LABEL used to describe the evidence.

The Curious Case of the Violent Video Game

For example – let's say that you enjoy playing computer games, but your mum is worried. She's seen news reports about a study which suggests that violent video games are connected with violent behaviour. She doesn't want you getting into fights or into trouble with the police. So she wants to stop you playing games.

How to deal with this? Well, you could stamp and shout. You could try tricksy debating tactics, like a lawyer trying to win a case in a courtroom. Yell 'objection!' a few times, that sort of thing.

Or you could act like a Truth Detective. That means asking questions. Let's look at those labels more closely. 'Violent video games', 'connected' and 'violent behaviour' . . . what do they really mean? Too often, we see the labels but we do not observe.

For example, does a 'violent video game' mean Minecraft, or Pac-Man, or Fortnite? Maybe your favourite game is Minecraft. If so, you know that it's mostly about exploring and building stuff (which is what you'll tell your mum) but you also know that it can sometimes be violent, too. One of the most popular early arcade games, Pac-Man, involved creatures running around eating each other. It sounds horrific but it was just little coloured shapes moving around a maze, chomping on everything in their path. Nobody thinks Pac-Man is really a violent game. Most people would say that Fortnite is violent, but there are more horrific games than that. So when the researchers studied violent games, what did they study? Pac-Man? Minecraft? Fortnite? Something *really* nasty?

What about this phrase 'connected with' violent behaviour? What does that mean? Do they mean that the kids who play violent games are also the kids who get into fights? That might not mean much – perhaps another of those causal forks:

Let's put this question to the experts. Scientists who research this question understand that this causal fork is a problem, so sometimes they will run carefully controlled laboratory experiments where people are randomly chosen to play gentle creative games or violent games, and are then tested to see if they act aggressively afterwards.

But how do you measure 'violent behaviour' in a laboratory? Nobody actually gets into a fight in a science laboratory![13] Some studies do something quite strange: they invite people to add really spicy hot sauce to someone else's drink. The idea is that if you're feeling more aggressive, you'll add more hot sauce. Does that seem weird to you? It seems weird to me. But some

[13] *Unless it's a superhero movie or spy thriller, in which case a fight in the mad scientist's underground lair is pretty much a certainty. Take that, Dr Octopus!*

researchers think it's a good way to measure aggression. And if people are over-generous with the hot sauce after playing a violent video game, well . . . ***MAYBE* VIDEO GAMES CAUSE VIOLENCE?**

This is all very interesting. The labels – 'violent', 'aggression' – they matter, don't they? So it's a question worth asking your mum.

- **Did the researchers find that people who play Minecraft every day for a year tend to get in trouble with the police?**
- **Or did they find that people who play Fortnite for thirty minutes in a laboratory then like to prank other people with big doses of hot sauce?**
- **What did the researchers actually do?**
- **And what did they find?**

Serious researchers disagree about whether violent video games cause problems, prevent them or maybe do nothing much at all. You and your mum can't solve a question that researchers have been arguing over for more than twenty-five years. But you can at least have a sensible conversation about what those researchers have found. And maybe you can strike a deal: you get to play Minecraft as long as you promise not to touch the hot sauce.

The Case of the Billionaires on the Bus

A few years ago, a well-known charity published a claim:

The wealthiest eighty-five people in the world had as much money as the poorest half of the world's population. You could fit all those billionaires on a single London bus, yet between them they had more money than billions and billions of people. It was a shocking number. The claim was published on the front pages of newspapers around the world, leaving the charity's workers high-fiving each other to celebrate how much attention they had received.

As Truth Detectives, what should we do? **CHECK THE LABEL.**

The first thing to check is: what do we mean by 'more money'? Let's compare two friends, Jill and Ted.

Jill has a regular babysitting job and makes £20 a week, 50 weeks a year.

She gets 20 x 50 = £1,000 a year.

Ted gets £3 a week pocket money 50 weeks a year.[14]

He gets 3 x 50 = £150 a year.

So who has more money? Jill, right? A lot more money.

---

[14] *Why not 52 weeks a year? I don't know. Maybe he doesn't get pocket money on holiday. Maybe he loses his allowance twice a year. Maybe the arithmetic is easier if it's 50 rather than 52, OK?*

But wait a moment. Jill enjoys going out for bubble tea with her friends. She often buys stuff for herself or gifts for others. Right now, she's spending money as fast as she earns it and has no savings.

Ted, meanwhile, is saving up for a games console. He's a patient fellow and has been saving all year, so now he has £150 in savings.

So who has more money? Ted, surely? He's got £150 and Jill doesn't have anything.

Wait, wait, wait. It can't be true that Ted is richer than Jill, while Jill is richer than Ted. Can it? Actually, it can be true. The problem is that words such as 'richer' or 'more money' seem simple but can mean different things. Let's look a bit more closely.

If by 'richer' you mean 'earns more', then Jill is richer than Ted. (Jill has more **INCOME**.)

If by 'richer' you mean 'has more saved up', then Ted is richer than Jill. (Ted has more **WEALTH**.)

So who is richer? Jill has more income, or money coming in. Ted has more wealth, or money saved up. (It's like Jill is taking a shower in money and it's pouring all over her, while Ted has filled a bathtub with money with a slow drip, drip, drip.)

The charity talking about the billionaires on the bus was talking about wealth. By that standard, Ted is richer than Jill. In fact, he's richer than a billion Jills put together, because Jill has zero wealth and a billion times zero is still zero.

Hm . . . a billion Jills put together. Doesn't that remind you of something? The charity complained that a busload of billionaires had **more money than billions of people put together**. But if those billions of people are people who have **zero wealth** like Jill then that isn't very surprising. Even Ted has more wealth than billions of Jills put together – and Ted, remember, still doesn't have enough money to afford that games console he wants . . .

If we want to understand the situation of the world's poorest people, it might be useful to look at their income as well as their wealth. Some people are so poor that they have less than a dollar a day to live on – people like the Kabura family in Burundi. We met them on Dollar Street in chapter three, and they make just $29 a month for a family of five. There are about 700 million people in the world in a similar position to the Kabura family, living on an income of less than $1.90 a day (this is awful, crushing poverty – although as we'll soon see, things used to be much worse in the past). Imagine trying to live on that! The Kabura family have low income and low wealth.

THE HUNDRED-BILLIONAIRES

Nobody knows exactly how much money the richest people in the world have, partly because they usually keep it a secret, and partly because it changes from day to day as money sloshes around. But some newspapers and magazines make lists with their best guesses. One recent list reckoned that there were four people with more than a hundred billion dollars each:

- **JEFF BEZOS, THE FOUNDER OF THE SHOPPING WEBSITE AMAZON**
- **ELON MUSK, THE BOSS OF THE ELECTRIC CAR COMPANY TESLA**
- **BERNARD ARNAULT, WHO OWNS LUXURY BRANDS IN FASHION, PERFUME AND CHAMPAGNE**
- **BILL GATES, FORMER BOSS OF THE SOFTWARE COMPANY MICROSOFT**

M0N3Y

Several other people were just under the hundred-billion-dollar mark – such as Mark Zuckerberg of Facebook, the investor Warren Buffett and the boss of a variety of Indian businesses, Mukesh Ambani.

Did you notice, by the way, that they were all men? What do you think that tells us about the world?

I prefer the Forbes Fictional 15 – a list of the richest people in novels, films and TV shows, including:

- **WILLY WONKA, CHOCOLATE FACTORY OWNER**
- **BRUCE WAYNE, AKA BATMAN (NO UNDERPANTS VISIBLE)**
- **SMAUG, A DRAGON**
- **TONY STARK, AKA IRON MAN**
- **MR MONOPOLY, THE GUY WITH THE TOP HAT ON THE MONOPOLY SET**
- **LARA CROFT, THE TOMB RAIDER**
- **JABBA THE HUTT, STAR WARS CRIME BOSS**
- **THE TOOTH FAIRY, ALTHOUGH SURELY HER FORTUNE IS IN TEETH, NOT CASH?**

M0N3Y

Either way, the richest people have a **HUMONGOUS** amount of money, and the poorest people have almost none. So what do we learn by breaking down the label 'more money' into 'wealth' and 'income'? I think we learn something important. The story about the eighty-five billionaires – one double-decker bus's worth – having more wealth than the poorest half of the world's population? That story suggests that if you took wealth away from a few very rich people you could solve global poverty overnight.

But if you look at the same numbers with the label 'income', the problem looks different. The super-rich have a lot of income, but not enough to lift the spending power of the poorest people in a way that will last. After all, there are eight billion people in the world. If you had eight billion dollars – which is **A LOT OF MONEY** – then you could only give everyone one dollar each and your money would be gone.

One billionaire who decided to try to do something about global poverty has come to the same conclusion. Bill Gates was for a long time the richest person in the world. He set up the Bill and Melinda Gates Foundation with the aim of 'fighting poverty, disease and inequity around the world'. ('Inequity' is a fancy word for things not being fair.) But if he had so much money, why didn't he just give it away to poor people? Well, the Foundation has spent more than $50 billion since the year 2000. That's just $6 per person on the planet. If Bill Gates had just handed out cash to people, that $6 would not have been enough to make a difference for more than a few days.

So instead the Gates Foundation has spent money on projects such as vaccines and libraries. Some people think this work is brilliant. Others think the Gates Foundation is spending money on the wrong things (and that, in any case, nobody should have that much money to spend). But one thing is clear: even $50 billion isn't enough to change the lives of eight billion people if you hand it out as cash.

So what should we do about global poverty? That's not a question I can answer for you, but it's a question you might feel better able to answer for yourself now. Could we take the money away from the rich and give it to the poorest people? Sure, we could: but we'd need to find a lot more rich people. Even the eighty-five richest billionaires between them don't have enough. We might need to start taking money from the *millionaires* too – there are about fifty million of them around the world, and between them they really *do* have a lot of money. But they might not be so happy . . .

Or maybe, like Bill Gates, we should be spending money to try to end poverty in other ways. It's not a problem anyone can solve easily. But you see the problem more clearly when you look at it both with the label 'wealth' AND with the label 'income'.

1) Observe the label on the data. What do they mean by 'violent video game'? When comparing rich and poor, are we comparing their wealth or their income?

2) It might seem boring to fuss about the details of the label – but it's actually the most interesting part of many statistical stories. What exactly is being said? How exactly do we know? If you don't ask these questions, you don't learn about that weird thing with the hot sauce.

3) When Holmes told Watson that he had seen the stairs, but he had not observed them, he was urging Watson to PAY ATTENTION. The world is full of interesting details. Do we notice them or not?

4) You might want to build up a tolerance for hot sauce. You never know when some weird researcher is going to sneak some into your drink in an experiment about video games.

ASK WHAT'S MISSING

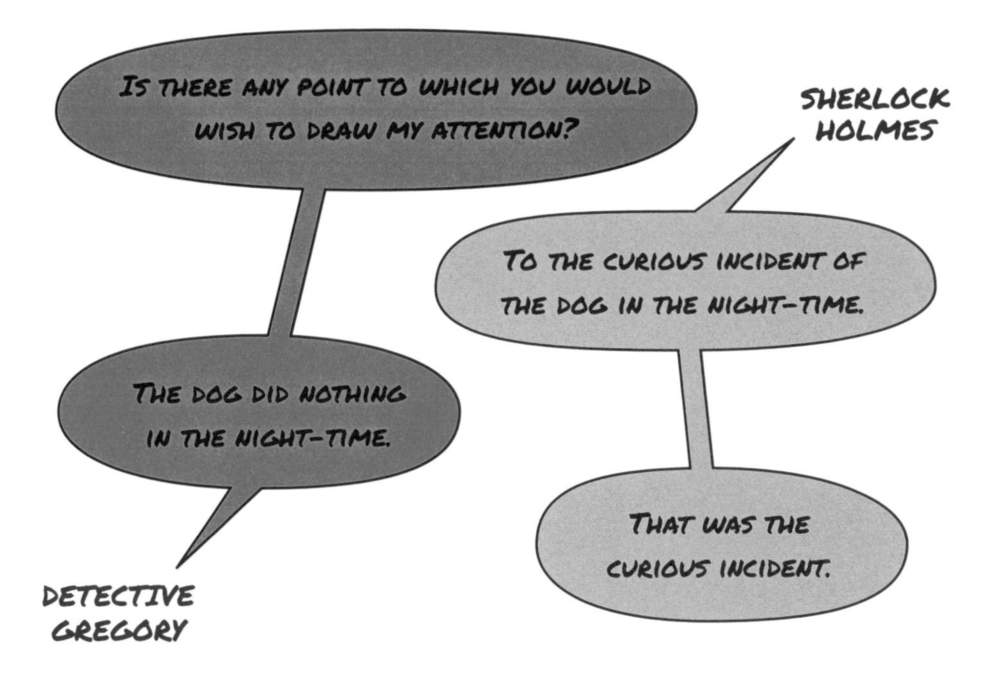

This dialogue is from one of the most famous detective stories ever written, 'Silver Blaze' by Sir Arthur Conan Doyle himself, published in 1892. Holmes is asked to help solve a double crime: the famous racehorse, Silver Blaze, has been stolen from the stables in the middle of the night, while Silver Blaze's trainer is dead, apparently murdered. Holmes makes a brilliant deduction by observing something that didn't happen: the stable dog did not bark: 'Obviously the midnight visitor was someone whom the dog knew well.'

To be a top-class Truth Detective, you need to pay attention not only to the things that are happening right in front of your nose, but also to the things that are happening out of sight – or not happening at all. Like the stable dog that did not bark, sometimes the evidence that is missing is the best evidence of all.

The Curious Case of the Prophetic Poop

A few years ago, a TV show in Norway announced a sort of fantasy football competition, except with no footballs and a pooping cow.

In fantasy football, you try to pick real football players who will play well in the real football league over the next few months. Those players go on your fantasy team – and if they do play well in reality, your fantasy team scores lots of points. What makes it hard is that you can't just pick all the best players, because they're too expensive and your fantasy team has a budget. You have to find the players who will play very well, but for some reason aren't too expensive. This is easy if you can see into the future – otherwise, not so much.

Now, the TV show's competition was actually a fantasy *investing* competition, where you had to pick Norwegian companies instead of football players. But the basic idea of the game was just the same: find picks that are cheap but which will surprise everyone with how well they do.

The TV show invited some interesting people to compete in this contest. There was an astrologer – someone who believes that by looking at the movement of the stars, they can forecast the future.[15]

Competing against the astrologer was a pair of professional experts: their job, day in and day out, was to try to figure out which companies are going to do well. 'The more you know, the better you'll do,' they said.

---

[15] *I don't understand how that would work, but people think astrologers are fun, so he was on the show.*

Hm – maybe.

The astrological fortune-teller and the professional experts were joined in the contest by two beauty bloggers. They might have been very good at make-up and creating helpful tutorials online, but they were the first to admit they knew nothing about fantasy investing. They hadn't even heard of the company names – and now they were meant to pick the best.

The presenters of the TV show also entered the competition, choosing a few of the companies they thought would do best.

But the most unusual competitor was called Gullros. Gullros was a big, beautiful, brown-and-cream coloured . . . cow. The TV producers marked out a white grid of twenty-eight squares on a field, labelling each square with the name of one of Norway's twenty-five biggest companies. Then Gullros and some other cows wandered on to the grid . . . and pooped all over it. Whichever grid squares had the biggest piles of steaming cow pats, those were the companies that Gullros and her herd had selected. When asked for an explanation of her strategy, Gullros replied, 'Mø.'[16]

So how did the competition play out? The astrologer did worst and the beauty bloggers did best – even though the beauty bloggers admitted they knew absolutely nothing. In the middle were the experts, who knew a lot, and Gullros the cow, who – let's be honest – was making choices by randomly pooping in a field.

---

[16] *This is Norwegian for 'moo'.*

What this really tells us is that trying to make money by seeing into the future of companies over the next three months is really just a guess. It's pure luck.

Except . . . EXCEPT . . . the presenters of the TV show suddenly revealed that they had done MASSIVELY better than everyone else. They had made almost as much money as the experts, the beauty bloggers and the pooping cow put together. But if the contest is basically pure luck – so lucky that a pooping cow can do as well as an expert, and a beauty blogger can do even better – then how had they done this?

It is a **VERY MYSTERIOUS CASE.**

But the answer is this: the TV presenters hadn't just entered the competition once. Secretly, they'd picked twenty different combinations. Imagine that they'd written each combination down, then put it in an envelope. Then when the time came to announce the winner of the competition, they flicked through the envelopes to choose the one they now knew had done best. Then they quietly dropped the other nineteen envelopes into the recycling bin.

It sounds outrageous! But it's really no more outrageous than . . . well, than everything we're about to hear about. It turns out that revealing ONLY the winners and hiding everything else is VERY common in life. And once you understand that, you can understand everything from how to do magic . . . to how to protect a plane from being shot down.

How to Toss a Coin and Get Heads Ten Times in a Row

The magician Derren Brown once performed a simple but amazing television stunt. He took an ordinary coin and flipped it into a glass bowl. The coin came up heads. He picked the coin out and flipped it into the bowl again. It came up heads again. He did it again, and again, and again. Heads each time. In fact, the coin came up heads ten times in a row!

Now, like many stage magicians Derren Brown is a master of illusion. He could have sneaked in a fake coin with two heads or fooled our eyes in some other way. But he didn't. The coin was perfectly normal. So was the flipping and the glass bowl in which the coin landed. The coin flip really did produce ten heads in a row.

WHAT ARE THE CHANCES OF THIS?

Not high. The chance of getting heads is 1/2. The chance of two heads in a row is 1/4. (This is because there are four possible combinations: heads then tails, tails then heads, tails then tails, or heads then heads – and only one out of the four is the one we want.) The chance of three heads in a row is just 1/8. The chance of four heads in a row, 1/16. The chance of ten heads in a row? 1/1024. If you repeated your series of ten flips 1,024 times, you'd expect to get ten heads in a row just once, purely by luck.

So how did Derren Brown achieve this incredible trick? Simple. He did exactly that: repeated the coin flips over and over and over again, thousands and thousands of times, until after hours of trying, he finally got ten heads in a row. The only piece of deception? The cameras filmed him doing this for hours, but they only broadcast the ten successful flips. Ta da!

It's not the world's most spectacular magic trick, but it is a magic trick with an important lesson for any Truth Detective. When we're being shown evidence, we need to ask not only, 'What does this evidence teach us?' but also, 'What evidence is missing?' Sometimes, as with the dog that did not bark, something did not happen and that's an important clue.

At other times, as with Derren Brown's coin flip, or the TV presenters trying to see into the future, something DID happen but we weren't shown it. That's an important kind of clue, too – if we can figure out what has been hidden from us.

TRUTH DETECTIVE

During the Second World War, a mathematician named Abraham Wald was asked to help the US Air Force decide how to reinforce their planes. Planes were returning from battle full of bullet holes in their wings. The planes could do with some armour plating! But the Air Force couldn't put armour everywhere – it would be too heavy. Very few planes had bullet holes in the flight deck or the engine. So maybe they could armour plate only the wings and leave the engine and flight deck unarmoured?

Abraham Wald disagreed. He pointed out that the air force couldn't see all the planes that were hit. They only saw the planes that were hit *but still got back safely*. Lots of planes were hit in the flight deck or the engine, he guessed – but those planes hardly ever got home. The ones hit in the wings often did.

So, said Abraham Wald, do the opposite. Leave the wings unarmoured and protect the engine and the flight deck instead.

The Case of the Blockbuster Potato Salad

If you had an idea for a cool new product, where would you go to get the money to help you produce it? Perhaps you could win a talent competition, discover a pot of gold or ask your parents REALLY nicely? But these are all long shots.

For many people these days the answer to their investment and money woes is Kickstarter – a website that lets people pledge money to support games, movies, books, comics, gadgets or other wonderful things. The inventors get publicity and money to turn their dreams into reality. The backers get the pleasure of feeling involved and, often, an early copy when the product is ready. The creators of the 'Pebble' smartwatch once raised $10 million on Kickstarter. A board game called 'Frosthaven' raised $13 million. Then the writer Brandon Sanderson announced that he was going to publish a series of fantasy novels, and he raised $15 million in a single day, breaking all of Kickstarter's records. But perhaps the most spectacular Kickstarter campaign ever was Zack 'Danger' Brown's efforts to pay for . . . a potato salad.

As a joke, Zack posted: 'Basically I'm just making potato salad. I haven't decided what kind yet.' He announced that he would do this if he raised just $10. Without offering much except a 'thank you', it was unclear whether anyone would send anything, but they did. He raised more than $55,000 from nearly seven thousand amused strangers who just liked the fun of sending a few dollars to some joker on the internet.

$55,000 is a lot of money – more than most people earn in an entire year. But with Kickstarter as a platform, Zack raised money to make surely the most lucrative potato salad in history![17]

When you hear about the $55,000 potato salad – not to mention the money being made by novelists and board game designers – doesn't it make you want to invent something and put it on Kickstarter? A board game would be cool, and there's no need to be greedy. You don't need $13 million. Just $1 million would do! Or if you need money faster than that, why not whip up some food? It doesn't have to be potato salad. It could be a bowl of cereal with a little sugar on top. Or perhaps a tomato ketchup sandwich? Let your cooking skills run wild and wait for tens of thousands of dollars to roll in!

Alas, I have bad news. Zack Brown may have raised $55,000 for his potato salad, but that doesn't mean you'll raise $55,000 for your ketchup sandwich. There's one very important thing missing from these exciting stories of Kickstarter success – all the stories of Kickstarter failure. A website named 'Kickended' collects these stories. A woman who wanted to design a swimming costume.

---

[17] He donated some of the money to charities fighting hunger, and he used the rest to throw a potato salad party for hundreds of people. Zack made several different kinds of potato salad for the party. Some used mayonnaise. Some used vinegar, the way they do it in Germany. I like the vinegary potato salad. Do you?

Later Zack shared his favourite potato salad recipe: 'One pound of potatoes, two ounces of mayonnaise, one ounce of sour cream, one ounce of MontAmoré cheese (or mozzarella as a substitute), one ounce of basil pesto, and then mix in the desired amount of pancetta (or bacon as a substitute) and sundried tomatoes with a splash of apple cider vinegar, black pepper and kosher salt.'

A man who wanted to travel around Scotland taking nice photographs. And two brothers from New York state who decided they wanted to film themselves doing **REALLY SCARY** trick-or-treating at Halloween, terrifying their neighbours with horrible costumes. They only wanted $400. And if you can get $55,000 for a potato salad, how hard could it be?

$55,000

But none of them got a penny – not from their friends, not from their siblings, not even from their own mothers. And it turns out that this isn't unusual. There's only one Zack 'Danger' Brown, raising $55,000 for a joke project. But there are more than fifty thousand Kickstarter projects that, like the trick-or-treaters, never got a single pledge of support. And on Kickstarter, failed projects – projects which don't reach their funding targets – are more common than successful ones.

This should teach us a lesson about much more than Kickstarter projects. Think about someone who's good at sport. Who comes to your mind? Maybe a footballing star like Kylian Mbappé. Or a brilliant young tennis player such as Emma Raducanu. Perhaps a basketball legend like LeBron James? Or maybe you're thinking of the Korean video-gaming star Lee Sang-hyeok – better known as 'Faker'. All inspiring people who get paid to compete – but of course most people who are good at sport don't get paid. They just play as a hobby. And even among people who get paid to play football or tennis or basketball or the computer game *League of Legends*, most of them aren't global stars. Of course, you know this already! But it's easy to forget, because it doesn't quite feel true. You'll read more stories about Emma Raducanu – and see more pictures, and watch more matches – than about all the millions of tennis enthusiasts put together.

The same thing is true of musicians, or writers, or social media influencers on TikTok or YouTube. You will see only the most exceptional – usually the exceptionally good, sometimes the fascinatingly bad, but always the unusual cases. That's partly because TikTok and YouTube have computer programs which tend to show you videos they think you'll like, based on what you've already watched. But it's also just arithmetic: one person with a hundred million views on YouTube is getting twice as many views in total than a million people with fifty views each. When you look at YouTube, you're much more likely to see that one person sucking up all the attention, and so when you think 'YouTube creator' you think of them, rather than the millions of creators with channels that almost nobody is watching. But the story is really just the same as Derren Brown tossing over a thousand coins but only showing you the time he got ten flips in a row. Remember when I told you about the TV presenters making twenty different attempts to win the forecasting competition against Gullros the pooping cow – and then only showing the best one? I said it sounded outrageous. But it's really no more outrageous than trying to figure out whether football is a good career by looking only at Kylian Mbappé, or whether to armour plate aeroplane wings by looking at the planes which safely return home, or whether to launch a project on Kickstarter by looking at the $55,000 potato salad.

What ELSE Is Missing?

We've learned about what we might miss when we focus only on what's in the shiny spotlight and ignore what's in the shadows or is kept secret from us. Now it's time to look at another blind spot.

Invisible Women

One possibility is that the people who collect the data don't try hard enough to include everyone or to ask questions that are relevant to everyone. For example, many famous psychological studies only used men in their experiments. Many new medicines were tested only on men, not women. Sometimes the researchers meant well, hoping to protect women from dangerous side effects; at other times they just didn't seem to think women were interesting. But the effect is that there was – and is – a big gap in our understanding.

TRUTH DETECTIVE

Caroline Criado Perez is a writer and campaigner whose work has transformed the way that many people think about women and data.

Her early campaigns focused on symbols: why were there so many statues of men and so few statues of women? And most of these were statues of queens and of females representing symbols like 'liberty' and 'justice' – the famous Statue of Liberty shows the goddess of liberty. But there weren't many statues of real women who had done inspirational work in science, politics, medicine or the arts. What about the brilliant mathematician Emmy Noether, or the campaigner for women's votes Emmeline Pankhurst, or the poet Emily Dickinson? (And that's just the women called 'Em' for short.)

Why were there no women (except Queen Elizabeth II) on banknotes? These campaigns won a lot of attention, and some changes, too: after initially refusing, the Bank of England announced that it would put the face of the novelist Jane Austen on the £10 note.

Then Criado Perez turned her attention to *data*. In a book titled *Invisible Women* she showed that the statistics we gather which are supposed to represent all people often only represent men. Sometimes this is because researchers only studied men. Sometimes it is because the way the data were gathered did not easily represent women's lives. The book attracted a lot of attention and won prizes. Many statisticians and data scientists are starting to realise they need to ask better questions in order to represent everyone.

Another problem is when survey questions are designed with men in mind. One survey in Uganda in Africa asked people about their main occupation. Most men replied with their job; many women replied to say their main occupation was as a wife and mother. When the survey was changed to ask about *all* jobs and responsibilities, women often added that they had a paid job too. Asking a better question revealed that

MILLIONS MORE

women had jobs. The older statistics with the old question had missed all these working women.

The Case of the Incredible Spreading Football Game

Have you noticed that football games have a tendency to spread all over the school playground? Caroline Criado Perez did. That's all very nice if you like to play football, but if you prefer other games – or if you're a football-loving girl and the boys won't let you play – then what can you do? What often happens, says Criado Perez, is that the football players (mostly boys) take over the space, while others (often girls) end up pushed into little corners.One alternative is to deliberately design school playgrounds with multiple spaces, reserving some places for football and other places for different games, from cartwheels to climbing to 'let's pretend'. Is this fairer? Does this mean that the girls are more active and get more space to play? We don't know. Why don't we know? Because we haven't yet collected good data about the playground problem.

If you had a chance to redesign your school playground or your local park, how would you do it? What sort of information would you collect to find out if everyone was getting fair use of the space?

1) When you're looking at a big success story, ask yourself whether you've also seen the failures. They might give you a very different picture.

2) Remember both the trick-or-treaters and the potato salad before you decide there's an easy way to get rich.

3) It's easy to imagine that the numbers are giving us every clue. But some clues are missing. Ask yourself what – and who – the data aren't showing you.

4) In a competition to see into the future, never challenge a pooping cow.

MAKE THE RIGHT COMPARISIONS

Money to the Moon and Back

More than forty years ago, the then-president of the United States, Ronald Reagan, gave a speech about the national debt of the US. The national debt is the total amount of money that the government has borrowed, and in 1981, the US national debt was about to hit a very large number: $1 trillion.

$1 trillion!

WOW! THAT'S HUGE!

But *how* huge? President Reagan tried to explain:

'A trillion dollars would be a stack of thousand-dollar bills sixty-seven miles high.'

Ever since then, people have been talking about big numbers using the 'stack of dollar bills' method. For example, Jeff Bezos, the billionaire founder of Amazon, has so much money that it

would be a stack of dollar bills 11,000 miles high. Wow! More recently, the US national debt exceeded $30 trillion – that's a pile of ten-dollar bills that would reach almost to the moon. Wow wow wow!

Except – do these comparisons really help? You know that the moon is a long way away, so you know that a pile of ten-dollar bills stretching out beyond the moon must be a huge number of ten-dollar bills. But you already knew that, right? You don't need to know much maths to know that $30 trillion is LOTS.[18]

And what if I used a different comparison? What if I said that the pile of money stretched into space, instead of to the moon? What if I said that the pile of money stretched to the sun, instead of to the moon? Would it make a difference to how you felt?

[18] And another thing - how many dollar bills are there in a pile, say, 1 metre high? A thousand? A million? You need to look it up before you have any idea! (It's a bit less than ten thousand.)

Maybe not. It all feels like, well, a big number. But there's a huge difference. Space is often reckoned to be 62 miles away – that's 100 kilometres, so people picked it as a nice round number. The moon is almost 240,000 miles, or over 380,000 kilometres. That's MUCH further. And the sun? The sun is almost 100 million miles or 150 million kilometres.

This really isn't helpful. 'Stretching to space' feels like 'stretching to the moon' feels like 'stretching to the sun'. But the difference is between 62 miles and 100 million miles. That's huge! Obviously there's a big difference between 62 and 100 million – 62 seconds is (of course) just over one minute, while 100 million seconds is more than three years. Or if I said I was going to give you some money for a birthday present, 62 pence isn't much, but 100 million pence is a million pounds. These are **HUGE DIFFERENCES**.

But the difference between 'into space' and 'to the sun' isn't nearly so clear. At first these comparisons involving stacks of money reaching into space seem very clear and vivid. But actually, they don't help us see clearly. They're not *meant* to help us see clearly. Instead, they're designed to catch the attention of our silly old Brain Guards and get them excited or angry. They're false trails, distracting us from the truth with vivid but meaningless comparisons.

We can do better – and if you're going to be a smart, savvy Truth Detective, you need to know how to make the right comparisons.

Good comparisons help us see the world more clearly. Bad comparisons leave us very confused. So what makes for a good comparison? Instead of measuring the US debt in terms of piles of dollar bills reaching to the moon, why not measure it in . . . dollars per person?

The US debt is, very roughly, about $100,000 a person. That's a lot! For many grown-ups that might be enough information to understand the situation. But we could make it even more vivid – it's very roughly what the average American earns in two years.

Two years of income! You can now think about what that would mean for you personally. How much do you earn in two years? If you get £5 pocket money every week, two years is about 100 weeks so that's £500. Imagine that you accidentally broke a £500 game console and your mum told you that you had to pay for a replacement out of your own pocket money – you know, just putting every penny **FOR THE NEXT TWO YEARS** into the project. Gah!

These comparisons take longer to make and maybe they aren't as eye-catching as talking about piles of money stretching to the moon. But they do help us track down the truth of the case.

The most helpful comparisons connect something you know well with something you don't. For example: how big is a dinosaur? The silly comparison is to look for a huge number – for example, you could say that a T-Rex weighed about as much as fifty million

matchsticks – which is true! But it's not really helpful. Nobody has a good idea of how much a matchstick weighs, other than 'not much'. So this comparison is really just saying 'one very heavy thing weighs as much as fifty million very light things'. It's so unhelpful I feel stupider just reading it.

It's much better to make comparisons that use familiar things. A T-Rex weighs about as much as four cars, and it's longer than a double-decker bus.[19] You know that a car weighs a lot, and that a bus is long. And now you can start to imagine what it might be like to see a T-Rex stomping down your street towards you. Forget fifty million matchsticks – RUN!

Landmark Numbers

If a good comparison connects something you know to something you don't, you need to have a useful collection of stuff you know. In fact, part of the Truth Detective's toolkit should include a collection of **LANDMARK NUMBERS**.

The writer Andrew Elliott popularised the idea of a landmark number. Here are a few examples:

---

[19] *And if the double-decker bus has the eighty-five billionaires on it, the ones from chapter five, then WOW. WOW WOW WOW. I wonder who would win in a fight between a T-Rex and eighty-five billionaires? What do you think?*

LANDMARK NUMBERS

- THE POPULATION OF THE UNITED STATES IS 330 MILLION PEOPLE. THE POPULATION OF THE UNITED KINGDOM IS 65 MILLION. THE POPULATION OF THE WORLD IS NEARLY 8 BILLION

- NAME ANY PARTICULAR AGE UNDER THE AGE OF SIXTY. IN THE UK, THERE ARE NEARLY A MILLION PEOPLE OF THAT AGE

- THE DISTANCE AROUND THE EARTH IS ABOUT 40,000 KILOMETRES OR 25,000 MILES. IT VARIES DEPENDING ON WHETHER YOU GO AROUND THE POLES OR AROUND THE EQUATOR, BUT NOT MUCH

- IT'S ABOUT A 400 MILE DRIVE FROM EDINBURGH TO LONDON. IT'S NEARLY A 3,000 MILE DRIVE FROM NEW YORK TO SAN FRANCISCO

- A BED IS 2 METRES – OR 7 FEET – LONG. THIS HELPS YOU VISUALISE THE SIZE OF A LARGE ROOM: HOW MANY BEDS IS THAT?

- THE PRICE OF EVERYTHING MADE IN THE US IN A SINGLE YEAR, ALL ADDED UP TOGETHER, IS ABOUT $25 TRILLION (OR $25,000 BILLION). IN THE UK, IT'S ABOUT £2.5 TRILLION, OR £2,500 BILLION

- 31,543 WORDS: THE LENGTH OF THIS BOOK

- 381 METRES: THE HEIGHT OF THE EMPIRE STATE BUILDING (IT'S ALSO ABOUT A HUNDRED STORIES)

You don't need to remember all of these. In fact, you don't need to remember ANY of them – you can always look them up in a book or online. Personally I like to carry a few of these landmark numbers around in my head. It's helpful, when I hear an unfamiliar number, to compare it to one of the landmark numbers I have in my head.

Remembering landmark numbers helps you make good comparisons. And good comparisons are one of the very best clues we have to help us understand the world.

The Puzzle of the Unobservant Granny

Whenever I used to see my grandmother, she'd exclaim, 'Goodness me, how you've grown!' It was a bit embarrassing. But I guess it was true. But my friend's gran never said such a thing to him. Was it because he wasn't growing?

Not at all: he was growing just like me. But his gran never said anything about it because she never seemed to notice.

So here's the puzzle: how come my grandmother always noticed that I'd grown, but my friend's gran never did?

The answer is simple. My grandmother lived a long way away, so I didn't see her very often. In between visits, I *had* grown. But my friend's gran lived in a flat next door to his house. She saw him almost every day. Did she ever say, 'Goodness me, how you've grown since yesterday!'? She did not. (So if you don't want your relatives to make a fuss about how much you've grown, go and see them more often.)

If you check for clues every day, you'll see different things than if you check for clues once a year. While my grandmother missed a lot of the day-to-day news that my friend's gran heard, my friend's gran also missed some clues that my grandmother saw. Every day, my friend was a tiny bit taller – but the increase in his height was always too small to see. But my own grandmother could easily notice that I was getting taller, because I might grow a few centimetres in a year.

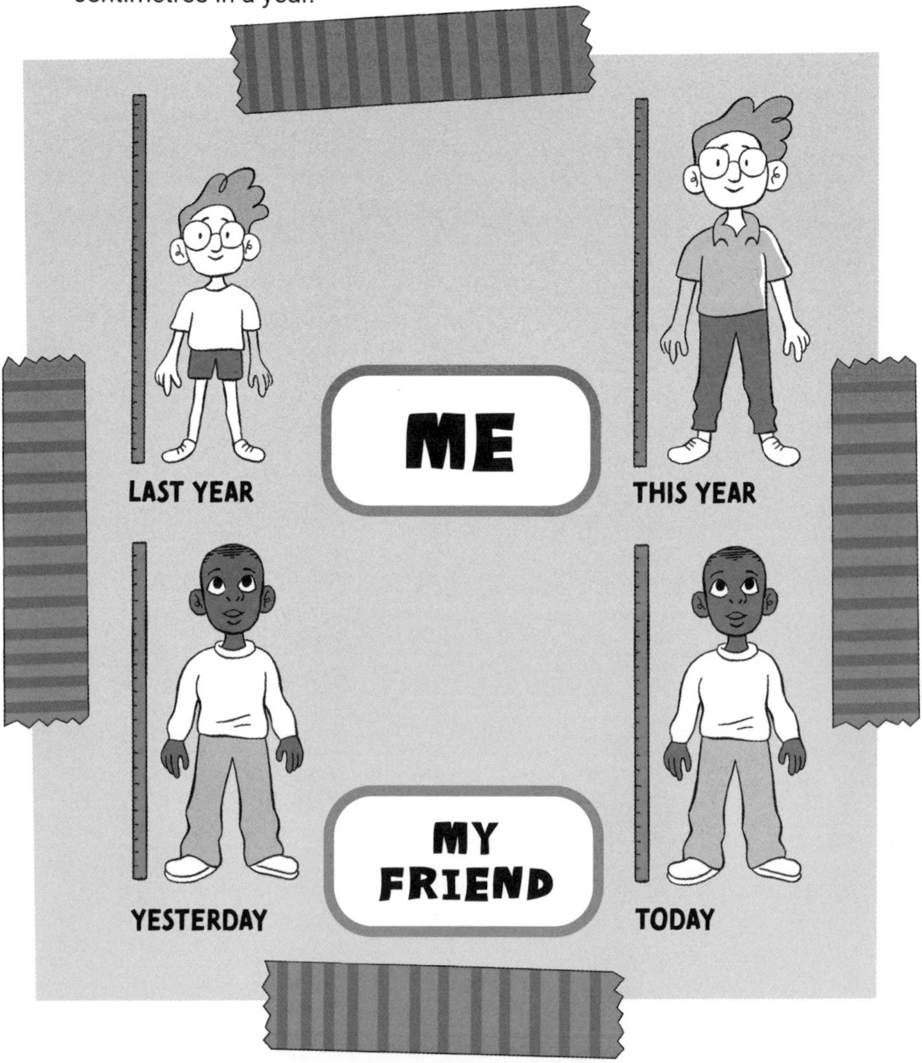

It's all about the **COMPARISONS** again. My grandmother was comparing my height one day to my height a year before. My friend's gran was comparing his height one day to his height the day before. And of course, his height never ever seemed to change. Once you think of this in terms of comparisons, you realise that sometimes when you look *less* often, you see more! The news that's published in an old-fashioned newspaper is, literally, yesterday's news: news stories about everything interesting that happened the previous day, packaged together, printed overnight and rushed to your door, or your local shop, early in the morning.

But not every newspaper is published daily. Websites and TV news try to update the news as it's happening. 'What's new?' often means 'What's happening right now?' or 'What is the most important thing that's happened in the last half an hour?'

Then there are newspapers in the UK such as the *Week Junior,* the *Economist* and *First News*, which are published once a week. And, just like my grandmother compared to my friend's grandmother, a weekly newspaper is going to ask different questions and get different answers, compared to a daily newspaper or an hourly TV news show. What counts as news depends on how often we ask, doesn't it?

We're often taught to think that faster is better. 'What's happening now?' is a different question to 'What happened this week?' or 'What happened this year?' – but it is not always a better question. Sometimes we learn more when we slow down.

THE FIFTY-YEAR NEWSPAPER

Imagine a newspaper published only once every fifty years. What would it talk about? A lot of the usual 'news' wouldn't make sense. You could forget celebrity gossip, the music charts or reviews of TV shows. Even more serious news about whether people were able to find jobs, or exam results, or even which politicians were winning elections – well, it would all start to seem rather trivial on a fifty-year timescale. The football pages would be pretty useless:

'MANCHESTER UNITED AND LIVERPOOL WIN A LOT.'

But before you dismiss the fifty-year newspaper as a silly idea, think about what sort of stories it *could* cover. What would the front page of the fifty-year newspaper say? One possible headline would focus on the miracle of safe childhood. It's upsetting to think about – but young children used to die. They used to die a lot.

Imagine a school classroom designed for thirty children, with thirty chairs set out. A hundred years ago, ten of those chairs would have been empty, because around the world, ten out of every thirty children born would not have lived long enough to ever go to school – there were too many diseases, and too few ways to treat them.

Fifty years ago, the situation was still bad, but much better: in a classroom for thirty children there would have been three or four empty seats.

Nowadays, there would be just one empty seat. Something which was once a tragedy that affected most families is now much rarer. And in developed countries the tragedy is more unusual still. This is amazing news! For a young child to die is one of the worst things in the world, but that terrible thing is almost ten times rarer today than a hundred years ago.

Daily newspapers wouldn't know how to report this good news story, because day by day it would never actually seem new. But slowly, slowly, slowly, it has become one of the most important (and wonderful) stories in the world. In our fifty-year newspaper it could be front-page news. And perhaps it should be!

Maybe you're thinking that the fifty-year newspaper would be more cheerful than ordinary news. I think you might be right, and maybe that's because when bad things happen, they often happen suddenly. A lot of good things (like developing cures for diseases, or discovering new scientific knowledge, or winning human rights for people who have been oppressed) take a long time. So if you look at the news every hour or every day, it will often seem like only bad things are happening. But more gradually – and perhaps also more importantly and powerfully – good things are happening too. They happen too slowly for ordinary news to pick them up – but if you step back and look at the longer sweep of history, lots of things are better for lots of people.

Think about poverty. How many people in the world live in extreme poverty? Picture the Kabura family in Burundi (we met them in chapter three) – they are an example of a family living in extreme poverty. Extremely poor people will often feel hungry. They probably have the most basic of places to live – perhaps a one-room hut, a dirt floor, no bed, no running water, no proper toilet and no electricity.

Fifty years ago, about half the population of the world had to live in such conditions. Nowadays, it is only one person in ten. That's a huge shift towards better, safer, more comfortable, more dignified living for billions of people. But how would you report it in a daily newspaper? You could write,

'AN ESTIMATED 154,000 PEOPLE ESCAPED FROM POVERTY YESTERDAY!'

That would be true. It would have been true every day for the last thirty years. But it would not be news.

THE PARADOX OF ZENO'S ARROW

This question of what counts as news – and what *doesn't* count – reminds me of a famous old paradox.

Zeno was a philosopher who lived about 2,500 years ago. In one of his most famous ideas, he asks us to imagine an arrow flying through the air. Now imagine freezing time for an instant and looking at the arrow hanging there. Is it moving? No, because it doesn't have any time to move in that moment. Nothing can move anywhere in zero time.

Now, says Zeno, isn't the journey of the arrow through the air composed of nothing but such instants? And if the arrow isn't moving during any of the instants, surely the arrow isn't moving at all?

People have been arguing about Zeno's paradox for a long time. If your initial reaction is, 'That's RIDICULOUS, of course when you shoot an arrow it moves', then . . . well, I agree, so there's a mistake in Zeno's logic somewhere.

For me, it all comes down to BAD COMPARISONS. If you compare the arrow's position now to the arrow's position at exactly the same time, of course you won't see movement. But if you allow some time to pass you can see the arrow moving. It's the same with climate change, with the escape from poverty, or even with my friend's gran not noticing that he'd grown. Look too often, without allowing enough time to pass, and you may miss clues that would be obvious if you were a bit more patient.

In the fifty-year newspaper, however, this mass escape from being poor certainly would be news.

'POVERTY BECOMES HISTORY!',

the fifty-year newspaper might write on the front page. Not quite true – there are still many poor people in the world. But nearly true – perhaps true enough for an excited newspaper editor to put it in a headline.

That's interesting, isn't it? On a daily or weekly newspaper, the escape from poverty isn't news. In the fifty-year newspaper, perhaps it would be the biggest story of all. And it's wonderful news, too.

Not all the news in the fifty-year newspaper would be good, however. The news about climate change would be bad. (Headline: 'GAH! BURNING COAL TURNS OUT TO BE A TERRIBLE IDEA!') Over the past fifty years, we have realised how much we can change the climate by burning coal, oil and other fossil fuels. And we have been able to measure the gradual increase in temperature. Daily or weekly newspapers find it hard to write news stories about climate change, because the climate doesn't change day by day – only the weather does. Often the stories are about scientific reports, or meetings to discuss the problem, or campaigners such as Greta Thunberg. That's fine – but for the real story, turn to the fifty-year newspaper.

TRICKS, TACTICS AND TOOLS

Understanding the truth is all about making good comparisons.

1) You'll often hear people making dramatic comparisons, like piles of dollar bills reaching to the moon. These comparisons might get your Brain Guard excited, but they are distracting.

2) A good comparison compares something you understand well with something you understand less well. It's how you make sense of the world!

3) You might want to make a mental note of some landmark numbers – from the population of the country you live in, to the length of a bed. Having these numbers in your head helps you think faster and smarter about what you're hearing. (Plus, you might be able to impress your friends and family with a few *did you knows*...)

4) Even if you don't want to memorise those numbers, you can always look them up to help you find good comparisons.

5) Remember the grandmother puzzle! If you keep looking at the same thing every day, you will miss important changes, whether it's the height of your friend, the screen of your smartphone, or the climate of the planet. Comparisons over a year, or ten years, or fifty years might give you better clues about the most important stories.

6) If you only memorise one comparison, perhaps it should be this: Batman weighs as much as 5,275 Freddos. (Unless it's LEGO Batman; a Freddo weighs as much as four and a half LEGO Batmen.)

SECTION THREE

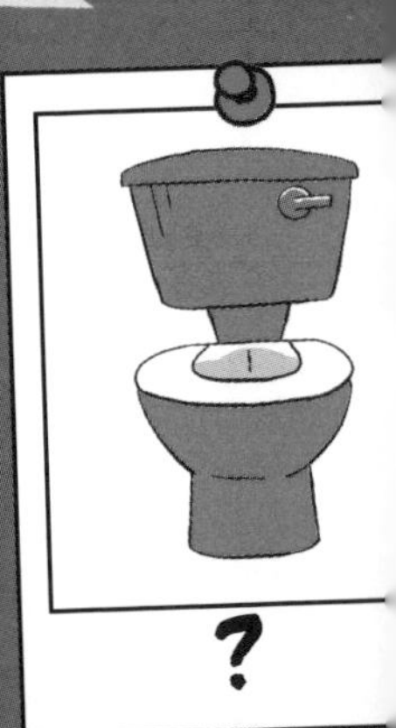

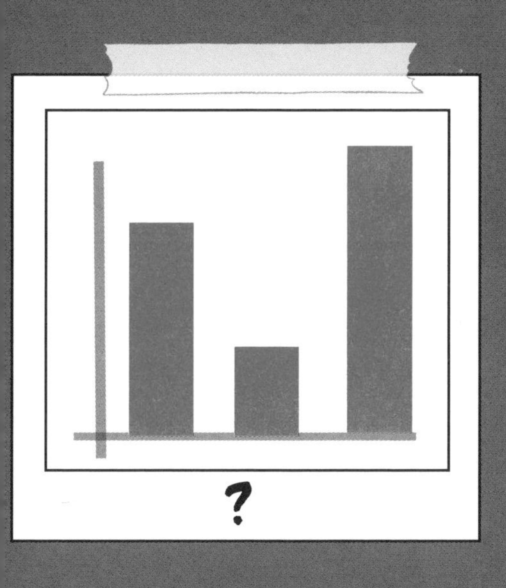

HOW TO CRACK DIFFICULT CASES

START A REVOLUTION WITH A PIE CHART

You've got the Truth Detective mindset, and you've got the Truth Detective skills. So let's talk about how to deal with some of the most challenging situations. What if you think you've solved a case, but nobody believes you? Or what if you can't even begin to investigate because there are no clues? Even these problems can be solved, so keep your magnifying glass within easy reach, and keep reading.

The Secret Life of Florence Nightingale

To most people, Florence Nightingale is famous as a nurse – the UK government even named emergency hospitals after her during the COVID pandemic. But to Truth Detectives, Nightingale is famous for another reason: she was the first person to truly understand that by turning data into pictures, you could not only understand the world, but you could *change* it.

But what change did Nightingale want to see? It all began in the wartime hospitals of the 1850s. The British Empire was at war with Russia, and Nightingale was in charge of some of the military hospitals.

Conditions were terrible. There was no equipment to treat the men, or even food to feed them. Nightingale called her hospital wards 'the Kingdom of Hell', and she wrote that back in England people could have little idea of how bad things were. Diseases such as cholera killed far more men than wounds from a bullet or a bayonet. Every day, Nightingale and her nursing team had to watch as soldiers died in front of their eyes.

After a few months, Nightingale got some support. A team from London arrived with a mission to thoroughly clean the hospitals, disinfecting the walls, clearing away piles of human poo – and even discovering and removing a dead horse from a large sewage pipe which was leaking into the drinking water for the largest hospital. Eurgh! After the cleaning team had done its work, the hospitals were cleaner, happier places – but Nightingale also believed that they were safer places, where fewer soldiers died.

When the war with Russia was over, Florence Nightingale returned to London. She had two missions: first, to understand the disaster in her hospitals; second, to persuade the entire world to learn a lesson.[20]

[20] When Florence Nightingale returned to London, Queen Victoria offered her some luxurious rooms in Kensington Palace, which would later become the official residence of the Prince and Princess of Wales, Prince William and Kate Middleton. But Nightingale instead chose to rent rooms at a cheap London hotel, where she set up an office and conducted her research and her campaigning. She felt that there would be too many visitors and too many distractions from her work if she stayed in a royal palace. If you were told you could live in a palace, imagine replying, 'Sorry - I don't want to be distracted from my work.'

Florence Nightingale's Truth Detective Army - and Their Enemies

The first mission sounds easy. Weren't soldiers dying because of germs? And didn't things get better because the cleaning team had cleared away the germs? Of course. You know that, and I know that. But in 1855, Florence Nightingale did not know that. Neither did anyone else, because the science of germs would not be established until some years later.

Instead, Nightingale gathered careful data about how many soldiers had died, and whether they had died of injuries or of disease. (This wasn't straightforward: until Nightingale came along, the British Army was careless about good record keeping, so nobody really noted the cause of deaths or even bothered to count the deaths properly.) The numbers backed up what we would now see as common sense: clearing away dead animals and piles of poo from the hospitals saved a lot of lives.

With a small team of Truth Detective friends, Florence Nightingale kept gathering information about disease and health in the Army and among ordinary people, too. What she found horrified her: a lot of soldiers were dying young, because of disease. The same thing was true in many communities across Britain, especially the densely packed cities. A lot of people said, 'Tough. That's life. People often die young.'

England's chief medical officer, Dr John Simon, described infectious disease as 'a cause of premature death in every civilised country' but added that such deaths were 'practically speaking, unavoidable'. This was the most senior doctor in the country! And he was saying, 'Oh well, people die of disease all the time, but there's nothing we can do about it, is there?'

Florence Nightingale was sure that was wrong. If Britain cleaned up its hospitals, and its military barracks, and the houses in which poor people were forced to live, then many lives could be saved. She had gathered some convincing clues during the war with Russia that suggested this had been true in the wartime hospitals. And if it was true in the wartime hospitals, wasn't it true elsewhere, too?

'Nature is the same everywhere,' explained Nightingale, 'and never permits her laws to be disregarded with impunity.' In other words, if a filthy wartime hospital killed soldiers, then filthy conditions back at home would kill many others too.

So Florence Nightingale's second mission – to change the world – meant that she was going to have to go into battle against Dr Simon and the other powerful and important men – the doctors and the generals – who thought that nothing needed to change. Lucky for Florence, she had a very unusual weapon up her sleeve: a pie chart.

TRUTH DETECTIVE

Florence Nightingale was born in Florence, Italy, in 1820. (Her sister, Parthenope, was born in Parthenope. I am not sure what their parents would have called them if they had been born in Barnsley and Birmingham.)

In an age when few people and even fewer girls went to a good school, Florence was lucky: her family was rich and her parents were determined to provide the best possible education. Florence was particularly interested in mathematics: at the age of nine, she gathered statistics about fruits and vegetables in the garden and organised them into a table of data. As a teenager she met important mathematicians who came for dinner at the family home – for example, Charles Babbage, who designed early computers. She eventually became a nurse – but after her wartime experiences, her love of carefully gathering numbers would become her superpower.

FLORENCE NIGHTINGALE

But she never forgot that those statistics described the deaths of individual soldiers in her hospitals. These soldiers often seemed forgotten amidst the disaster of the war, but Nightingale personally wrote a letter to every family of a soldier who had died. The big picture is important, but each person is important too. Nightingale knew that.

Florence became very ill during the war with Russia and nearly died at the age of thirty-five. She never fully recovered, and she conducted much of her campaigning work by writing letters from her bedroom. In the end, she lived to the age of ninety – long enough to see her ideas transform the world.

How to Persuade the Queen of England to Pay Attention

Nightingale's problem was simple: because she was a woman, people didn't take her seriously. She had a wonderful reputation as the saintly nurse who had tended to British soldiers during the war with Russia. She was perhaps the most famous woman in the British Empire, other than Queen Victoria herself. And she had some powerful friends – influential politicians and scientists. But at that time, she was a woman in a man's world. Just because Nightingale was a famous nurse didn't mean that the generals or the doctors would listen to her ideas. It was infuriating. But she had a solution. On Christmas Day in 1857, Florence wrote to a friend to explain how she was going to win the fight for ideas. She was going to turn her numbers into pictures. Her diagrams of data would tell a story that nobody could ignore. And she added that she would have her diagrams framed and hung on the walls of senior doctors and generals.

She would even send her pictures of data to Queen Victoria, as well as other kings and queens across Europe, the chief medical experts in the Houses of Parliament, and to every newspaper and magazine. Queen Victoria was busy and didn't read much. But Nightingale thought that the Queen might make an exception for her report: 'She may look at it because it has pictures.'

Making Numbers Look Beautiful

Pictures of data are very common now. You might have had to create bar charts or pie charts in school. Such diagrams fill encyclopaedias, decorate news stories and go viral on social media. No wonder: they seem scientific, but they look pretty. It seems like the perfect sweet spot between hard facts and decoration.

But back in the 1850s when Nightingale was fighting her campaign, statisticians would usually just write out huge tables, filled with numbers, which often looked boring and complicated. It was very unusual to draw a graph instead, but in doing so, the stats were brought to life and Florence Nightingale changed the world.

If you wanted to change something about the world, what would it be? What do you want people to do differently? Think about the information you might want to gather together. Maybe it's something everyday – like you think they should include more orange Smarties in each tube. Maybe it's a local problem, like the number of cars which drive through your neighbourhood each morning. Maybe it's something global, such as climate change or war. What numbers would you use – and how would you transform them into a persuasive picture?

LET'S SEE HOW FLORENCE NIGHTINGALE DID IT . . .

The Deadly Rose

Florence Nightingale's most famous graph is titled 'Diagram of the Causes of Mortality in the Army in the East', but is often just called the Rose Diagram. It wasn't the first ever data visualisation, but it was an early example – and a hugely influential one. It's been more than 160 years since it was created, and now data visualisations are everywhere. There are simple charts shared on social media, animated graphs, even three-dimensional interactive visualisations that you can move around inside like the world of a computer game. These graphs can show all sorts of data, from the serious (such as charts of COVID cases spreading around the world in 2020) to the fun (such as an interactive chart showing the shape and distance to the boundary of all the major cricket grounds in England and Wales, or a graph showing the distribution of all the different colours of chocolate in a packet of Smarties or M&M's).

Numbers come alive as pictures.

Nightingale's graph, which helped to start it all, was published in 1859, the year after Dr John Simon declared that death from infectious disease was unavoidable.

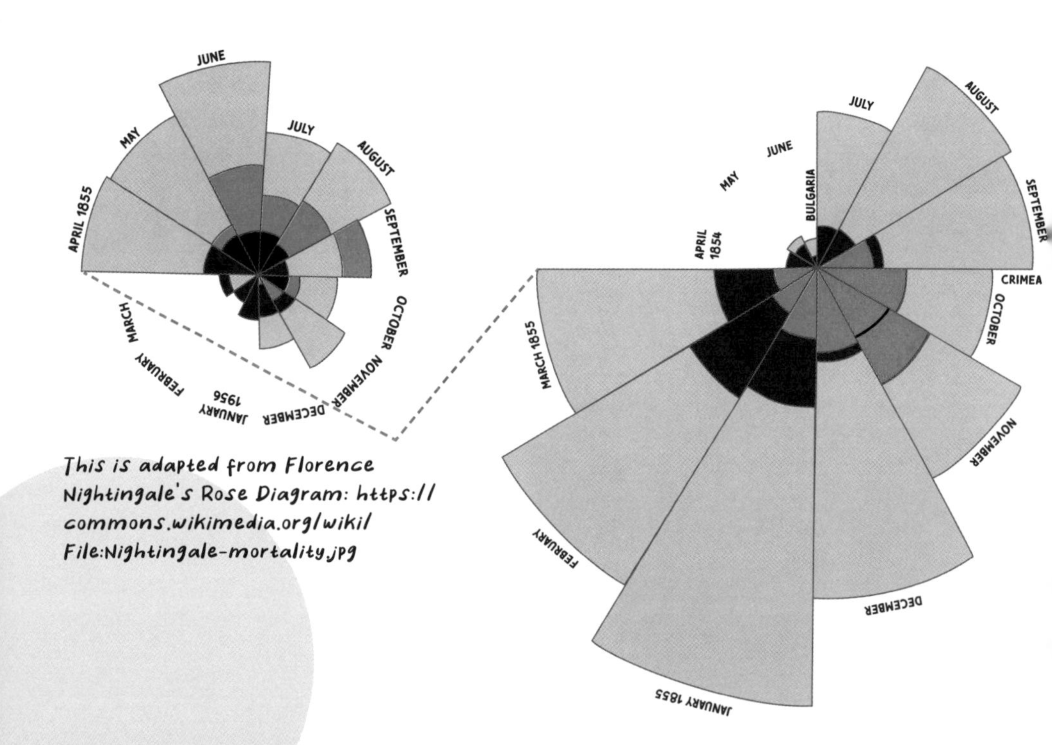

This is adapted from Florence Nightingale's Rose Diagram: https://commons.wikimedia.org/wiki/File:Nightingale-mortality.jpg

The diagram is a more complicated version of a pie chart. Each wedge in the diagram stands for a different month of the war with Russia, and because each of the two spirals contains twelve wedges, that's a whole year. In fact, the big spiral on the right is the first year of the war, and the little spiral on the left is the second year. The size of the wedges stands for something horrible: the number of soldiers who died that month. The orange wedges are soldiers who died of their wounds. The black wedges are soldiers who died in accidents. The grey wedges are soldiers who died of disease.

Straight away, you can see two things. First, disease was the big killer: far more soldiers died of disease than from a bullet or a sword wound. Second, most of the deaths happened in the first year of the war. Things were much better in the second year.

This was the story that Florence Nightingale wanted to tell: a story with two halves. The first half of the story was a tragedy, full of death caused by disease. The second half of the story was a heroic recovery: there were far fewer deaths. Deaths from disease were preventable! The two halves of the story were divided perfectly by the design of the graph.

And what else divided the two halves? **THE CLEANING TEAM**. Washing the hospital walls, carting away the poo, clearing dead animals away from the water supply.

The cleaning team arrived at the end of the first year of the war, which means that the two halves of Nightingale's diagram could easily have been labelled **BEFORE** and **AFTER**. The story could not have been clearer. And Florence Nightingale's enemies found to their horror that they were starting to lose the argument.

Graphs vs Brain Guards - Be Careful!

When you do your own work as a Truth Detective, be careful when you meet a pretty graph. Remember that some of these graphs are deliberately designed to fool you. Others are carelessly put together and are misleading by accident.

People make decisions very quickly when they see a graph – sometimes too quickly. One study found that people would form an opinion about a graphic within just half a second. That's not enough time to understand what the graph says, but it is enough time to think, 'What a mess,' or, 'Ooh, pretty!' Other studies have found that people are more persuaded by evidence if it comes in the form of a graph rather than a table full of numbers. Remember the Brain Guard? The Brain Guard really loves pretty pictures.

Because we quickly jump to judgement about graphs, it's important to slow down and follow the advice of this book. Ask yourself: is my Brain Guard being fooled by a nice picture? What's behind the numbers that make up this graph? Where is the lens pointing, and could it be pointing somewhere else? Are there numbers missing from the graph that should be there? Don't be fooled, because some graphs can save lives, while others can lead us astray.

Not All Graphs Tell a Story

If you want to persuade someone else of your case, a graph can help. As a Truth Detective, you've been learning to gather clues from the numbers all around you. Florence Nightingale was brilliant at carefully assembling numbers. But when trying to win her argument, she showed that she was brilliant at getting numbers to tell a story, too.

After all – the Nightingale Rose Diagram isn't a conventional way to display data. A much more common graph is a bar chart. But if you draw Nightingale's data as a bar chart, it just doesn't tell the same story.

This chart contains the same data as Nightingale's Rose Diagram. But here the impact is different. In fact, after you stare at the bar chart long enough you start to realise just how clever Florence Nightingale was. Sneakily clever, in fact. In the bar chart, you notice how bad things were in the coldest months – December, January and February. You notice that things were getting much better *before* the cleaning team arrived in March.

You might start to ask other questions like, 'Was it really the cleaning team that made the difference?' or, 'What if the disease was mostly caused by bad winter weather?'

Even though Nightingale was absolutely right – the diseases were caused by germs, and the cleaning team saved lives by cleaning

'This bar chart is based on the original by Hugh Small, published in his paper, 'Florence Nightingale's Hockey Stick: The Real Message of her Rose Diagram':
http://www.florence-nightingale-avenging-angel.co.uk/Nightingale_Hockey_Stick.pdf

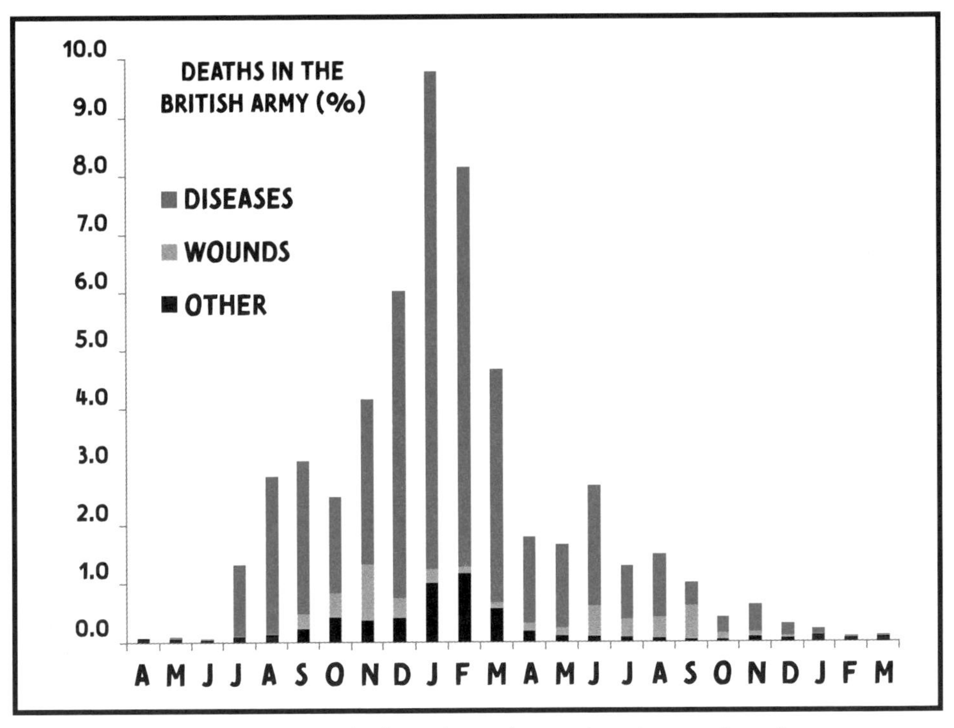

away those germs – the bar chart shows that the numbers by themselves weren't convincing enough. They were a bit too complicated. So she gave them a little help by plotting a graph that told a story. Can you blame her?

Nightingale won her argument. The British government passed new laws to make sure that people had cleaner water, cleaner homes and cleaner air. People started to live longer. Diseases were rarer. Scientists discovered germs, showing that many of Nightingale's ideas about good hygiene had been right all along.

EVEN DR JOHN SIMON QUIETLY CHANGED HIS VIEWS. THAT'S THE POWER A DIAGRAM CAN HAVE.

The right data can save lives. Richard Doll and Austin Bradford Hill showed that when they discovered the links between smoking and diseases such as lung cancer. But Florence Nightingale showed it too, a century earlier.

And in the next chapter, you'll find out how to make your own data when clues are scarce.

TRICKS, TACTICS AND TOOLS

CLASSIFIED

1) Graphs can attract attention very fast – and once you have that attention, you can use it to send a powerful message.

2) If you're drawing a graph, think about the story the graph is telling. (If your graph doesn't tell a story, maybe you need a better graph.)

3) If you're reading a graph, be careful! Your Brain Guard loves pretty graphs. Slow down and think.

4) Don't mess with Florence Nightingale.

HELP BUILD THE STATISTICAL RADAR

Information Is the Best Weapon

In 1935, Europe felt like a dangerous place. The terrible slaughter of the First World War was a recent memory, and with Adolf Hitler rebuilding Germany's military, many people were nervous that a second great war would come. (It did.)

So there was lots of interest in developing new weapons using the latest scientific ideas. The British Air Ministry wondered if it might be possible to develop some kind of 'death ray', shooting down incoming German bombers with the power of science![21] So the Air Ministry asked a scientist, Robert Watson Watt, whether it was possible.

Watson Watt posed an innocent-sounding question to his colleague Skip Wilkins: what if you had 4 litres of water, and you wanted to heat that water from 37 degrees Celsius to 41 degrees? Now, what if you were half a mile away or more – could you do it with radio waves and how much power would you need?

Skip Wilkins knew very well that an adult human body contains 4 litres of blood at a temperature of 37 degrees. He also knew that raising the temperature of that blood from 37 to 41 degrees might kill someone and would certainly make them faint. Skip was able to work out very quickly that Robert Watson Watt was thinking about using radio waves to create a weapon . . . **THE DEATH RAY!**

---

[21] *They even offered a grand prize for anybody who could zap a sheep at a distance of a hundred paces. Nobody claimed it.*

But the two men also agreed that the idea was pretty hopeless, because it would take far too much power to project a ray potent enough to actually knock out an incoming bomber pilot while he was at the controls.

But Skip Wilkins reckoned he could build something much better. Before long, the two men were hard at work on the alternative project. Instead of beaming death rays at incoming aircraft, they would send out a much weaker signal and then listen out for reflected signals as they returned. If they got it right, they could fire this radio wave off into the air, detect the echoes coming back and figure out whether there were incoming planes – and if so, how many there were, how fast they were going and where they seemed to be aiming for. That was much better than any death ray. Instead, it was information – early warning of enemy bombers approaching. And it worked. What Wilkins and Watson Watt had developed was soon given a name: radar.

It wasn't enough just to invent the technology: the British had to get organised. They set up a ring of radar stations codenamed 'Chain Home'. When Germany started bombing the UK in 1940, the radar stations provided early warning of the incoming attacks. The defending planes could be kept on standby until

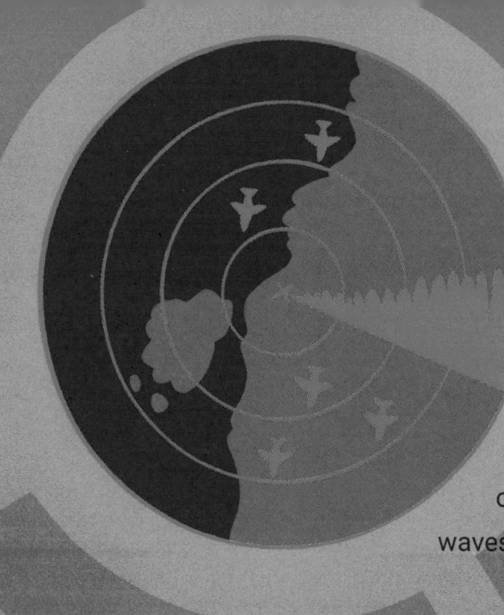

needed, then scramble into action at exactly the right moment and in exactly the right place. With assistance from radar, even a small force of defenders could repel large waves of attacks. And they did.

German scientists had also made a start on radar, but the German leader Adolf Hitler was much more interested in developing weapons to attack, not gathering information for defenders.

Radar was no death ray. Unlike bullets and bombs, it never directly harmed anybody. And yet many people believe that radar was the single most important technology in the Second World War! When a threat is approaching, it helps to be able to see exactly where it is.

Hitler made a serious mistake in not understanding how important a technology like radar could be. But our own leaders often make similar mistakes, believing that it's not very interesting or important to get good information. They're very wrong.

How to Save a Million Lives

In March 2020 it was becoming clear that the COVID pandemic was going to change the world. Just like the radar pioneers Skip

Wilkins and Robert Watson Watt decades before, two medical researchers had a clever idea about how to fight back. A lot of energy and attention was being put into the super-weapon against the virus: a vaccine. But like Wilkins and Watson Watt, these medical researchers had an alternative plan. And like Wilkins and Watson Watt, their plan involved producing better information.

One of the researchers was Professor Martin Landray. While riding a big red double-decker bus across London with a colleague, he discussed the terrible wave of illness that was coming fast, and he explained the problem: all over the world, people would soon be arriving in hospitals, desperately ill. And all over the world, doctors would try to help them by giving them medicine. But because COVID was a new disease, nobody knew for sure which medicines might help. And so patients would sometimes get better and sometimes get worse, and nobody would really know if any of the medicines were working. Landray teamed up with another professor, Peter Horby, to figure it out.

Horby and Landray had a surprisingly simple idea: get organised. Instead of doctors all over the place trying out promising medicines almost at random, doctors could team up together, using a computer to assign promising medicines *precisely* at random. When a patient came into a hospital with severe COVID, their details would be entered into a computer, and the computer would suggest one of four promising medicines, or sometimes a pretend medicine called a **PLACEBO**.

BEFORE

TREATMENTS ALMOST AT RANDOM

Under Horby and Landray's plan, almost the same thing was happening as before: there would be a bunch of doctors, a bunch of patients and a bunch of medicines that people were trying without really being sure whether they worked or not. But under Horby and Landray's system, because the computer was randomly assigning treatments and carefully keeping track of the results, medical guesswork turned into a **SCIENTIFIC EXPERIMENT** which would quickly discover which medicines worked and which didn't. And as more information was discovered, useless medicines could be stopped and new possible cures could be tried out.

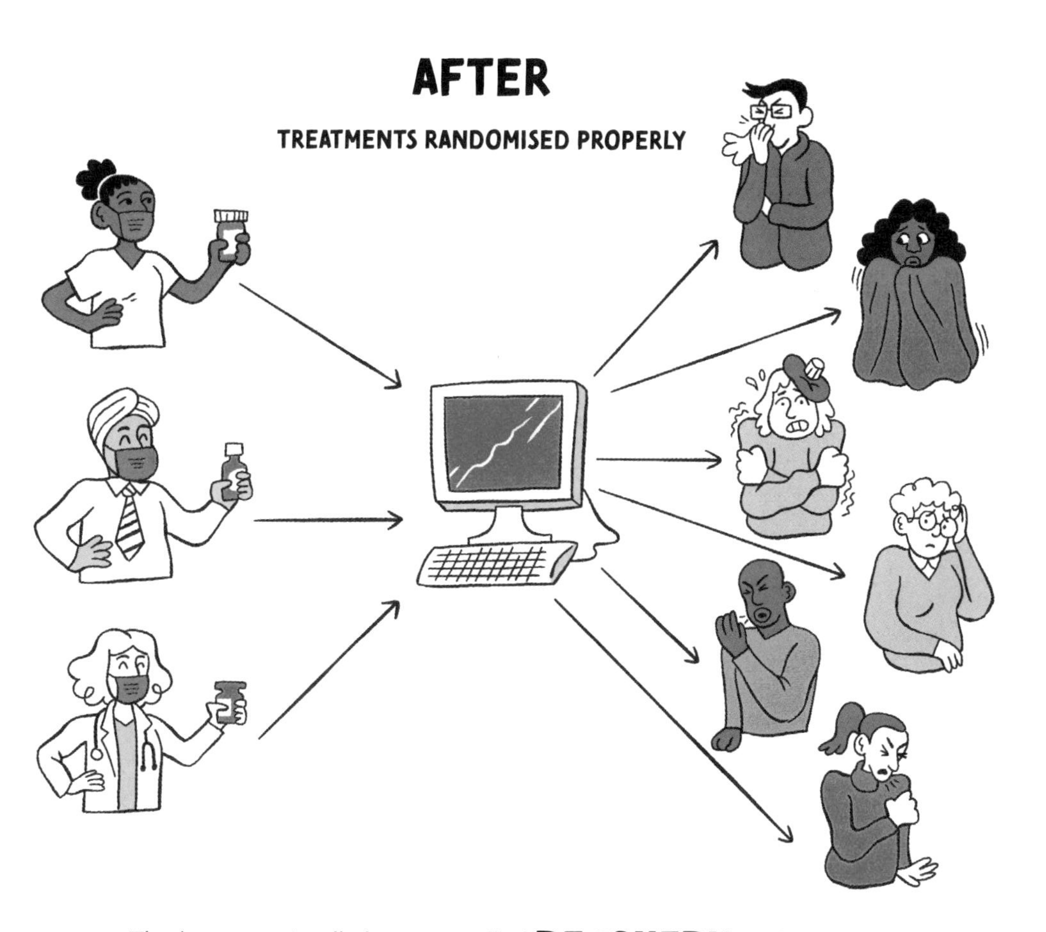

The 'get organised' plan was called **RECOVERY**, and the **RECOVERY** trial was set up in just a few days. Weeks later, they had results. There was one medicine that lots of people were using, partly because it had been praised by the then President of the United States, Donald Trump. The **RECOVERY** trial discovered that unfortunately it didn't work.[22] But another medicine worked incredibly well! Even better, it was a cheap pill, easy to make, affordable and available to almost any hospital anywhere on the planet.

---

[22] *Sad! But still useful. If you discover that something popular doesn't work, it saves the expense and side-effects of giving people a medicine that isn't helping them. And you clear the way to figure out what does work.*

Later, people calculated that this new treatment alone had saved the lives of a million people. And the **RECOVERY** trial kept running and kept investigating and discovering new treatments. In the first year of the pandemic, with vaccines barely available, Martin Landray and Peter Horby saved more than a million lives by organising what was already happening to produce much better information.[23]

Collecting good data can be a big, complicated project. But it's often much easier if you think ahead. Let's say you wanted to gather that information about the number of different coloured Smarties in a tube. You could buy a packet, open it and count them. But that doesn't give you much information. It's better to have a hundred tubes than one.[24]

So how do you get a hundred tubes of Smarties? Well, you could get other people at your school to count the colours in each tube they buy. You could set up an online spreadsheet where people type in their results. Or you could even build a three-dimensional Smarties graph at school, made out of transparent tubes – just add each colour to each tube and see the count increase . . . The point is, it's easier to do this when you get help from your friends and when you think ahead.

Of course, once you have the information, someone needs to

[23] I once had the chance to ask Martin Landray what it was like to have saved a million people's lives. He didn't boast. Instead, he mumbled that he didn't think it was quite THAT many.

[24] By 'better' I mean you get better data if you collect more examples. But obviously more chocolate is also nicer to have than less. Just don't make yourself sick!

present it in a way that is easy to find and understand – something Florence Nightingale understood very well. And if governments won't do that, some surprising Truth Detectives will sometimes step up and take responsibility – as we're about to see.

The Case of the Mysterious Data Website

While vaccine scientists worked to create and test vaccines, and the **RECOVERY** trial was quickly finding the best treatments for people in hospital, ordinary citizens around the world were hungry for information: how many new cases were there? How many new cases NEAR ME? How many people were in hospital? And later, when vaccines against the disease were developed, how many people have been vaccinated?

People in Australia had the same sorts of questions as everywhere else, and like everyone else, they would go online to find out more. Unfortunately, the numbers were often quite confusing. Different parts of Australia would report things in different ways, at different times and on different websites. One area might put a printable document online, while another posted numbers on Twitter. This made it very hard to compare the information coming from different places, or to explore the patterns in the numbers. So before long, Australians found themselves turning to CovidBaseAu, a website that was gathering together all of the confusing numbers in one place. Whatever questions people had, they could find the answers on CovidBaseAu.

This website pulled all the right numbers together in the same place and presented them clearly. More and more people started to use it to get their information. Newspapers, news websites and TV news would often mention CovidBaseAu as their source for information. But all the while, nobody suspected that behind these numbers there was an amazing secret.

Then one day, three teenagers – Wesley (fourteen), Jack (fifteen) and Darcy (fifteen) – posted a picture of themselves on Twitter, just after getting vaccinated.

'Today the three of us who run @covidbaseau, Jack, Wesley and Darcy, had our first dose of the Moderna vaccine. Thought this would be a good time to share who we really are. Thrilled that we will finally be included in our data!'

It was true. To celebrate being vaccinated, Wesley, Jack and Darcy announced to the world that they were the people who had set up the CovidBaseAu website!

It was an amazing story. Jack had started the project 'just for fun' and had been joined by Darcy (who had been programming since he was seven years old, and handled the coding) and Wesley (the all-rounder, producing graphics for social media). Like the ace Truth Detective Batman, they kept their true identities A SECRET. Everyone assumed that the website had been built by a team of adult experts – not by three schoolkids!

Wesley, Jack and Darcy won a lot of fans for their anonymous work, and even more fans once they revealed their true identities. One medical research organisation offered them all part-time jobs. The story has inspired a lot of people and can teach us a few lessons.

- **FIRST**, even if you're just three school friends, it's amazing what you can do if you try.

- **SECOND**, be a bit careful about just trusting any old website. CovidBaseAu presented good data, but it could easily have presented bad data instead. Nobody actually knew who was behind it. There are lots of websites or social media posts which say things that just aren't true. People share those lies anyway, often without thinking.

- **THIRD**, we should take numbers more seriously! It is incredible that three teenage boys could do a better job than the ENTIRE GOVERNMENT OF AUSTRALIA in pulling together reliable information and presenting it clearly. KIDS ONE – ADULTS NIL. That's great work from the boys. Still, isn't it a bit embarrassing that the government of a whole country couldn't do better?

The Data Crisis and How to Fix It

The Australian government wasn't the only one which struggled to collect and publish good information during the pandemic. Many governments did disappointing work. For example, in the US, health departments had such out-of-date systems that they were sharing data about COVID cases by fax.[25]

---

[25] A fax machine is such old technology that you might not even know what it is! Fax machines are like photocopiers connected by telephones. You can scan a piece of paper in one place, and the copy will appear somewhere else - even on the other side of the world. The technology is about a hundred years old, and it was popular in the 1980s and 1990s. But in the twenty-first century, it is much better to send data directly from one computer to another, rather than sending scans of pieces of paper.

In the UK, people in care homes were at very high risk of becoming seriously ill from COVID. But the government didn't actually know how many people were receiving social care in each area. In the United States, there was a similar problem – at the start of the pandemic, nobody even knew how many hospitals there were in the country.

That might seem strange – wouldn't it be easy to figure out how many people were receiving care or how many hospitals there were? Well, we don't know whether it was easy or difficult, because nobody had done it. Useful numbers don't just appear from nowhere and arrange themselves into neat rows and columns. Somebody has to do the work – collect the data (like Florence Nightingale did) and put it into a useful form (like Jack, Wesley and Darcy did) – otherwise we simply don't know what's going on.

Unfortunately, people very rarely pay attention to the importance of good information and often only notice when somebody surprising does something really cool – like Jack, Wesley and Darcy – or when something goes badly wrong.[26]

---

[26] What do I mean by 'badly wrong'? Oh, what about the time the healthcare system in England lost track of nearly 16,000 COVID cases? These were people who should have been warned they were ill and that they needed to stay at home to avoid infecting others. But they weren't warned, because their cases were automatically deleted (quietly, and without warning) when the computer program storing the data ran out of room! It was simply a case of bad computer coding; Jack, Wesley and Darcy would probably not have made that kind of mistake.

The COVID crisis has revealed a lot of problems in data collection. But we have learned lessons too. For example, governments are starting to realise that you can track COVID – and other diseases – by **POOP ANALYSIS**. People with a COVID infection have coronavirus in their poop, and the virus stays there for a while. So scientists go to sewage works, where all the poop from a particular area goes to be processed. The scientists take a sample of all the poop mixed together to see whether there's any of the COVID-causing coronavirus there and, if so, how much. It can provide early warning of a new coronavirus outbreak. After Gullros the Pooping Cow, this is a second victory for poop data!

Jack Monroe's campaign to produce a better picture of inflation for poor families is yet another example of problems in data collection. (You might remember it from chapter two.) For years and years, inflation had been very low and nobody had worried much about whether poor families had a different experience. But as soon as prices began to rise, Jack started to shout about the problem.

That's one thing we can all do: complain loudly if the data we need aren't available. But there's something else you can do:

GET YOUR OWN DATA.

Jack Monroe did that with her Vimes Boots Index. Jack, Wesley and Darcy did it when they turned an unusable pile of official numbers into a well-organised website that anyone could use.

How could you get your own data?

Well, let's say you think that the school dinners at your school aren't good enough – there isn't enough choice, there aren't good options for vegetarians, they serve lumpy custard.

What might you do about it?

GATHER THE EVIDENCE. Spend a week or longer noting the availability of different options. Once you have enough detail, you can start to look for sensible categories, for example: hot/cold; meat/veggie; lumpy custard/no custard.

ANALYSE. Are there any days where no vegetarian option is available? Are some days of the week particularly bad, or good? If you can read the patterns in the data, you might be able to spot a particular problem – or a solution.

COMPARE. Do you have a friend or a brother or sister at a different school? Do their school dinners work differently? Do they have more options? If every school is equally bad, you're going to need to start a national campaign. But if you can prove that your school is worse than others, you might get the head teacher to do something about it more quickly.

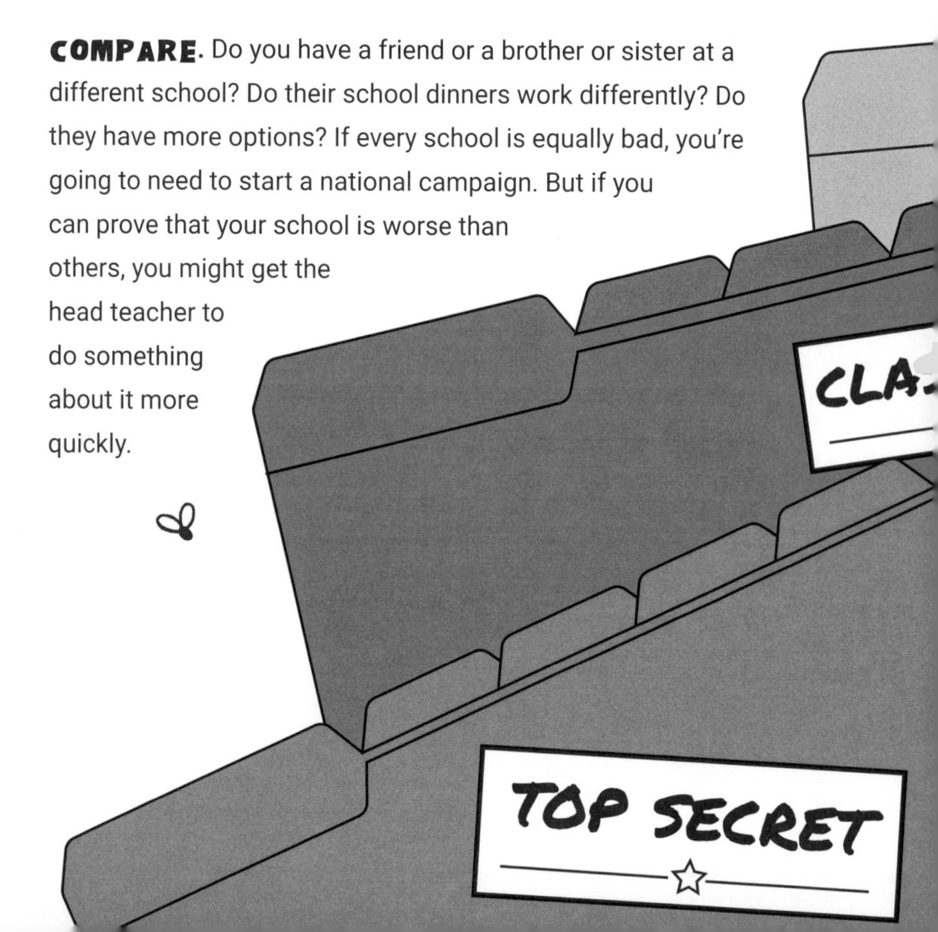

TRICKS, TACTICS AND TOOLS

1) Remember Skip Wilkins's insight: good information is the best weapon you can have.

2) Sometimes governments are so bad at assembling information that some teenagers can do better. If you are, or are planning to become, a teenager, this is a huge opportunity.

3) When nobody else is gathering good data, you can make a huge impression by gathering your own. Gather what you can, analyse it and make good comparisons, and before long you like Florence Nightingale, might provoke a revolutionary change.

4) If you ever do something that saves a million lives, don't boast.

SHARE YOUR CURIOSITY

Seeing Only Our Own Side

Many years ago, two scientists (Albert Hastorf and Hadley Cantril) showed a video of a university football game to some students. The students were from the two universities involved, so they strongly supported their own team and opposed the other side. This particular football game was bad-tempered and rough. There were lots of penalties. One team captain got a broken nose. The other got a broken arm! Since this isn't really supposed to be the sort of thing that happens at a football game, people argued about whose fault all the trouble was. But the students watching the game felt very differently, depending which side they were on.

The scientists asked the students some questions about what they had seen. At one university, more than half the students said the game had been fair – rough, maybe, but fair. At the other university, almost nobody said it had been fair. There was a similar disagreement about which side had started the rough play. People saw lots of fouls committed by the other team and far fewer fouls committed by their own team.

You're probably aware of this kind of behaviour yourself – especially if you've ever watched a sporting event with a friend who supports the opposite team to you.

But this doesn't just happen to sports fans. Inspired by the study of the football game, some scientists later decided to show people a video of a political protest. The video didn't give any clues about why people were protesting. And again, the researchers asked questions: were the protestors calm and peaceful? Or were they insulting, frightening, even violent?

However, before the video of the protest started, the scientists told a fib. They told some people that the protest was for a particular cause they strongly supported. Other people were told that the protest was for a cause they strongly opposed.

As you can guess, people saw very different things. If they supported the protest, they said the protest was peaceful. If they opposed the protest, they said they saw the protesters screaming, bullying and scaring people. Just as in the case of the football came, people saw totally different things depending on which side they supported. Their Brain Guards were hard at work, not just letting in or keeping out different ideas, but even influencing what people saw with their own eyes.

This is sad. It would be nice to be able to sit down and have a sensible conversation with people who disagree with us. But it's often hard, because both we and they have these lazy, emotional Brain Guards filtering what goes into our heads. If we watch the same video but see different things, how on earth can we talk about our disagreements without getting angry or confused?

Fortunately, there is a solution to this problem. Are you curious to know what it is? I hope so, because . . . it's **CURIOSITY.**

Scientists have found that curious people are less likely to leap to defend their own side of an argument. I'm not exactly sure why (although I am curious to know). It might be because when you disagree with a curious person, they might find your disagreement itself quite interesting, rather than threatening.

A usual argument might go like this:

What a terrible game - so many fouls and so much cheating.

I don't know why you're complaining – your team were the ones doing all the fouls!

What are you talking about? You must be blind or stupid. Anyone can see that YOUR team were the cheats.

And so on. Not very nice, and not very useful. Nobody changes their mind during an argument like this. But an argument with a curious person is very different.

What a terrible game - so many fouls and so much cheating.

It did seem bad. I wonder why there were so many fouls?

I think it all started with that terrible challenge by your team's captain - that should have been a red card.

Interesting. I don't remember it quite like that. Can we look at a replay? I'm interested to know what you thought was so bad about it.

Different, isn't it? At the end of the conversation these people might still disagree, but at least they're learning something rather than just contradicting each other. It's possible that one of them might actually change their mind, but even if they don't, it's a more friendly, more interesting chat. That's the double power of curiosity: it doesn't just help us change our own minds, it might help other people change their minds too.

Good detectives, from Sherlock Holmes to Miss Marple to Ottoline Brown, are always curious. When you're curious, you know that there's something you don't know: a gap in your knowledge. And so you keep your eyes open, alert for clues, always asking questions. Sherlock Holmes almost never made a mistake, but there was one case – 'The Adventure of the Stockbroker's Clerk' – when he was caught by surprise and somebody nearly died as a result. Why did Sherlock make this mistake? Because he stopped being curious for a moment: he thought he already understood everything about the case. He stopped asked questions. Very unusual! It was a mistake he only made once.

TRUTH DETECTIVE

Stephen Colbert seems an unlikely Truth Detective: he's an American comedian, well known for pretending to be a crazy, stupid and politically extreme TV personality.[27]

But Colbert understands the challenge of being a Truth Detective very well. He invented the word **TRUTHINESS** to describe what happens when we are sure something is true – and when we insist to other people that it's true – not because of clues or evidence, but because it just feels right.

The Truth Detective always seeks the truth – but our Brain Guards LOVE a bit of truthiness instead.

[27] But he is just pretending. Once upon a time I was a guest on Colbert's TV show. Backstage, he was very friendly. He explained, 'I'm going to be in character. And my character is an idiot. He knows nothing and he hasn't read your book.' Later, when he was in character, he yelled through my dressing room door, 'I'M GOING TO TEAR YOU APART, HARFORD!'

But Colbert isn't just a Truth Detective because he understands the difference between truth and truthiness. Because he makes politics funny, he's brilliant at inspiring curiosity. For example, politicians in the US get huge amounts of money to pay for their election campaigns, which often means they pay more attention to the people who give them that money than to ordinary voters. That seems . . . bad. But it's very confusing. It's hard for most people to understand where this money comes from and what the rules are.

Stephen Colbert helped to explain this problem in a brilliant way. He announced that he was going to run for president (in character, as an IDIOT) and asked experts to come on his comedy show and teach him how to raise money secretly that he could spend however he liked. Colbert's joke presidential campaign lasted for months, and the more people saw the outrageous things he was able to do with money, the better they understood the problem.

A study later showed that people who watched Colbert's show, *The Colbert Report*, had learned more about money in politics than readers of serious newspapers and magazines. Colbert's joke made people curious about something important, and because they were curious, they learned a lot.

The Secrets of the Universe (or a Flush Toilet, Anyway)

How can we encourage other people to be curious? Stephen Colbert was funny; that helps. But here's another trick that might help: ask them questions.

Let me start by asking YOU some questions.

Do you know how a flush toilet works?
What about a zip fastener?
Or a crossbow?

If you were to rate your knowledge about these things on a scale of one to seven, how would you rate it? If you ask people these questions, they often think they have quite a good idea. Then if you give them a pen and paper and ask them to draw a diagram, with explanations – they start to struggle. If I asked you to draw a diagram of a flush toilet and explain exactly how it works, how well would you do?

Try it now, before you read on . . .

Here are two explanations of how a flush toilet works. The first explanation might score a one out of seven on the knowledge scale – or maybe a two. At least this person knows how to work a toilet and what it looks like.

The second explanation, on the next page, is a seven out of seven. It contains all the important details about both the mechanics of the toilet and the scientific principles behind how it operates. (Which explanation was closer to yours? Do you think you scored a three? Maybe a six?)

1. THE FLUSH HANDLE IS CONNECTED TO . . .

2. A VALVE, WHICH RELEASES WATER FROM A STORAGE CISTERN INTO . . .

3. THE RIM OF THE TOILET BOWL. THIS MEANS THE WATER WASHES THE BOWL AS IT FLOWS IN.

4. THIS IS THE S-BEND, WHICH ALWAYS CONTAINS ENOUGH WATER TO PREVENT BAD SMELLS COMING UP FROM THE SEWER. AS MORE WATER FLOWS IN FROM THE CISTERN, THE WATER LEVEL RISES UNTIL IT REACHES THE LIP OF THE S-BEND. THIS CREATES A SIPHON EFFECT WHICH SUCKS MOST OF THE WATER OUT OF THE BOWL: THERE IS HIGHER AIR PRESSURE ABOVE THE BOWL THAN IN THE PIPE.

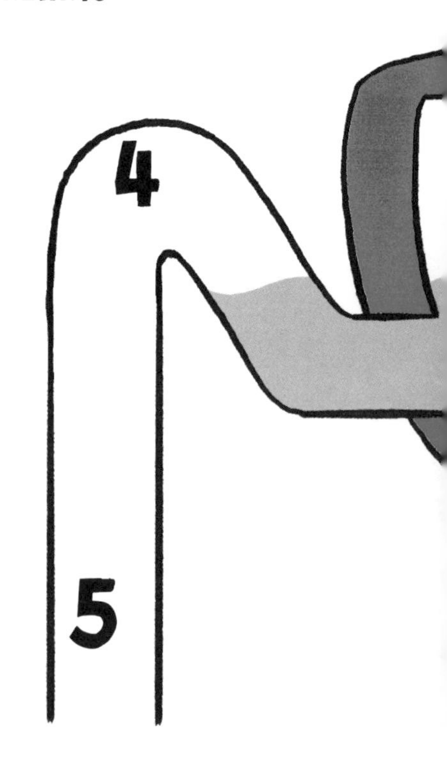

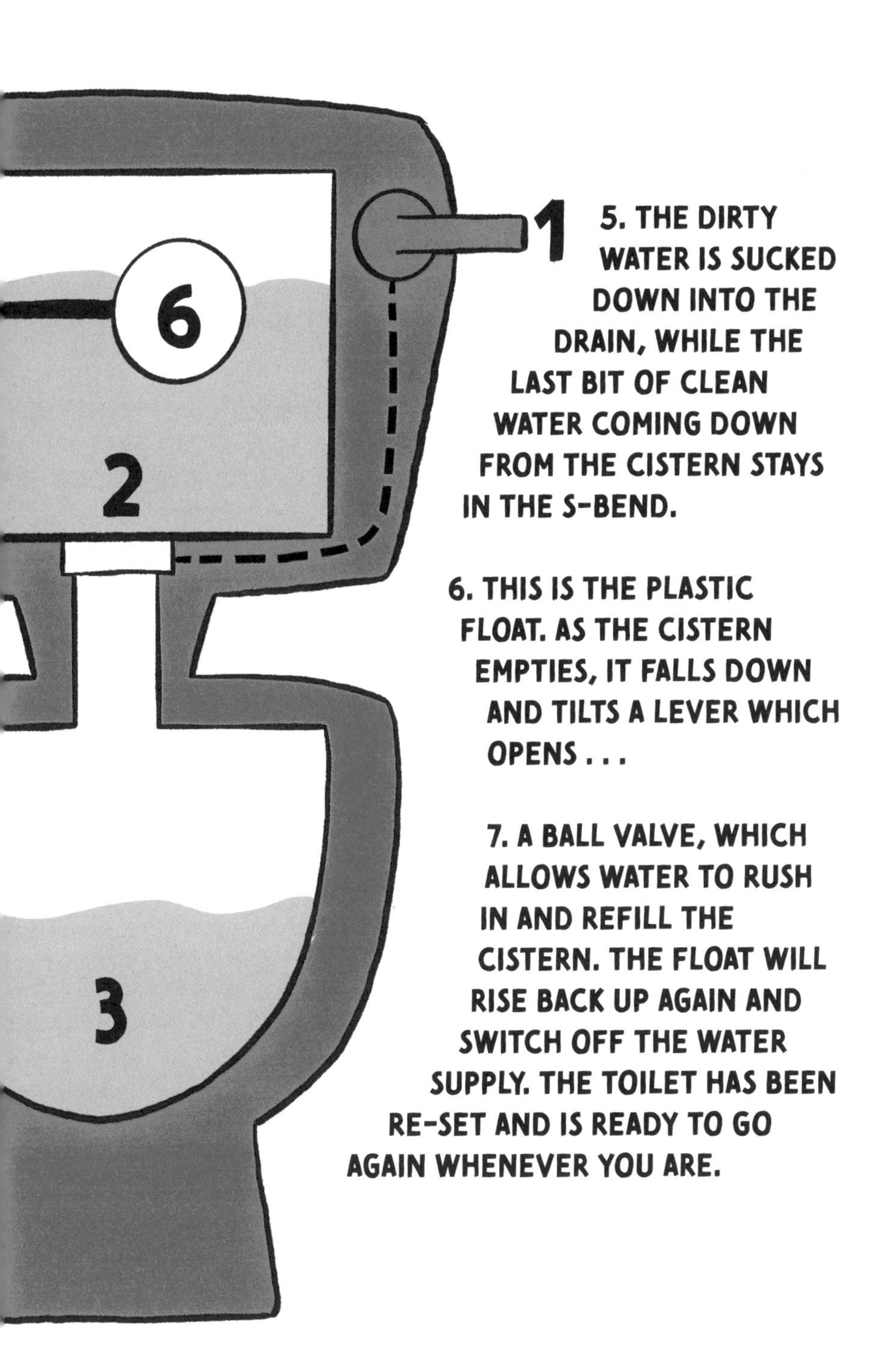

5. THE DIRTY WATER IS SUCKED DOWN INTO THE DRAIN, WHILE THE LAST BIT OF CLEAN WATER COMING DOWN FROM THE CISTERN STAYS IN THE S-BEND.

6. THIS IS THE PLASTIC FLOAT. AS THE CISTERN EMPTIES, IT FALLS DOWN AND TILTS A LEVER WHICH OPENS . . .

7. A BALL VALVE, WHICH ALLOWS WATER TO RUSH IN AND REFILL THE CISTERN. THE FLOAT WILL RISE BACK UP AGAIN AND SWITCH OFF THE WATER SUPPLY. THE TOILET HAS BEEN RE-SET AND IS READY TO GO AGAIN WHENEVER YOU ARE.

People can often be very stubborn in their views, insisting they know stuff that they don't. Sometimes that's easy to fix. If people are arguing about which footballer has scored the most ever goals, you can easily look it up on the internet and discover the truth . . .

But often people just won't admit that they're wrong. They won't even admit that they might be wrong. And here's where the zip fastener or the crossbow or the flush toilet can be magic. Because when you give someone a pencil and paper and ask them to explain it, first they realise that they don't know as much as they thought, and then they usually admit it.

I call this magic because it's so unusual for people to simply say, 'Oh, yes, I guess I don't really know what I'm talking about.' People are usually very confident, **ESPECIALLY** once they get into an argument with somebody. But if instead of arguing, you say, 'Please tell me more,' people may well realise that they don't actually understand as much as they thought they did.

This isn't just about zip fasteners and flush toilets. It turns out that the same thing is true of complicated political ideas. People will shout and yell because they support or oppose a particular policy, but if you ask them to explain how it works (not whether it's good or bad, but simply WHAT IT IS) then they will often start to struggle. And as they start to struggle, they also start to admit that maybe they shouldn't be quite so stubborn. They will start to learn that they didn't know quite as much as they thought.

(Of course, it's possible that they won't struggle at all, and that they know **A LOT**. That's fine. If you've asked a question to somebody who knows **A LOT**, then sit back and enjoy, because you're going to learn **A LOT** too!)

Asking questions about what other people think often gets them to be more open-minded and less over-confident. Even if it does neither of those things, asking such questions is polite and kind: it shows that you CARE what they think. You are more likely to have a good conversation and less likely to have an argument if you ask people friendly questions, then actually listen to their answers.

It's also just as important to ask yourself questions. Do I really understand what I'm talking about? Where are the gaps in my knowledge? What questions would I like someone else to answer? This sort of curiosity is all-important.

How to Be a Truth Detective

By now, you know a lot about how to be a Truth Detective. You've heard about the kind of gear you might want to wear, and the way your Brain Guard can get in the way of noticing the right clues. You've learned that you need to be smart and savvy. You've learned that statistics can be an important lens, like a magnifying glass – and that it matters where you point the lens. You've found that sometimes you need to pay attention to your personal experience as well as to the clues you're uncovering using the lens of statistics. And you've discovered that people sometimes criticise bad statistics as a way of discrediting good statistics, too.

You've developed important skills: observing the label; asking what's missing; making the right comparisons. And you've learned about gathering your own data and using graphs to make your case.

But this last lesson may be the most important of all. If you want to be a good Truth Detective, you need to be curious. If other people disagree with you, start by asking open-minded questions rather than by trying to persuade them. They might learn something. More importantly, **YOU** might learn something. And while it's easy to focus on what you think you know, it's more fun to explore what you **DON'T** know.

The world is an amazing place. It is full of puzzling cases. And as a Truth Detective, you get to explore every mystery. The wonderful thing about being a Truth Detective is not just that you get to figure out the truth. It's also that along the way, you're never bored.

GLOSSARY

CONFIRMATION BIAS: When we have an idea in our heads and we look for reasons that we're right, ignoring reasons that we might be wrong.

CORRELATION: When one thing goes hand in hand with another. For example, people who have large cars will often have lots of children. Correlations can be important clues, but they can also be red herrings. If you think the correlation is real, you still need to figure out why. Do you think large cars increase the number of children in a family? Or do you think people with lots of children decide to buy larger cars?

DATA: A collection of information, usually a collection of numbers. There's a big argument about whether 'data' should be singular (like 'information') or plural (like 'numbers'). Should we say 'the data is telling us who secretly runs the Red Hand Gang' or should we say 'the data are telling us who secretly runs the Red Hand Gang'? Which is right? Either is fine. (You might want to flip back and forth between 'data is' and 'data are', just to confuse people.)

FAKE NEWS: Stories that look like real journalism but which are just made up in order to fool people or to get clicks on the internet. Real journalism isn't always correct, but journalists have to follow some standards of checking their facts. Fake news sites don't bother. BE SAVVY! But don't just watch out for fake news. Also beware TRUTH VILLAINS who tell you that real news stories are fake news. Remember the lesson of Darrell Huff – if you can get people to doubt the truth, that's just as powerful as getting them to believe lies.

OFFICE FOR NATIONAL STATISTICS: In the UK, this is a government agency responsible for gathering and analysing data about the country. The US has a different system in which there are lots of different government agencies working to produce different statistics. The biggest are the Census Bureau (which among other things counts every person in the country once every ten years) and the Bureau of Labor Statistics (or BLS). The BLS calculates inflation in the United States. (By the way, 'bureau' is a fancy word for 'office'.)

PLACEBO: A fake treatment, designed to have no effect. In a medical trial, people often feel better just because they feel they are getting treatment. So when researchers are trying to measure whether a new medicine works, they will often compare it to people receiving a placebo pill instead of people receiving no treatment at all.

STATISTICS: Numbers that have been gathered in an attempt to measure or count things in the world around us; or the science of organising and examining those numbers.

STATISTICIANS: People who collect and analyse statistics. Truth Detectives will sometimes collect their own data, but often they will use statistics produced by expert statisticians for everyone's benefit.

TRUTHINESS: When something feels true, when we want it to be true, but there's no good evidence that it's actually true . . . that's truthiness. (The word was invented by the comedian Stephen Colbert.)

ACKNOWLEDGEMENTS

If you want to be a Truth Detective, you'll need the help of many people!

I'm so grateful to everyone who has helped me grow and learn as a writer, a journalist and a professional nerd – as well as to the scholars, writers and activists on whose work I so often rely.

They include Ruth Alexander, Anjana Ahuja, Mohit Bakaya, Julia Barton, Ananyo Bhattacharya, Esther Bintliff, Michael Blastland, David Bodanis, Innes Bowen, Alberto Cairo, Andy Cotgreave, Kate Crawford, Caroline Criado Perez, Kenn Cukier, Ryan Dilley, Andrew Dilnot, Anne Emberton, Richard Fenton Smith, Baruch Fischhoff, Walter Friedman, Alice Fishburn, Hannah Fry, Kaiser Fung, Dan Gardner, Courtney Guarino, Andrew Gelman, Bruno Giussani, Ben Goldacre, Rebecca Goldin, David Hand, Dan Kahan, Daniel Kahneman, Paul Klemperer, Richard Knight, Kate Lamble, Bill Leigh, Denise Lievesley, Mia Lobel, Eileen Magnello, Viktor Mayer-Schönberger, Charlotte McDonald, Lynn McDonald, Lizzy McNeill, David McRaney, Barbara Mellers, Errol Morris, Will Moy, Nicola Meyrick, Jack Monroe, Jake Morrissey, Terry Murray, Sylvia Nasar, Cathy O'Neil, Onora O'Neill, Neil O'Sullivan, Zoe Pagnamenta, Matty Prinku-Wright, Robert Proctor, Nithya Rae, Jason Reifler, Alex Reinhart, Anna Rosling Rönnlund, Max Roser, Hans Rosling, Alec Russell, Benjamin Scheibehenne, Hetan Shah, Janelle Shane, Jackie Shost, Hugh Small, Lucy Smith, David Spiegelhalter, Matthew Syed, Philip Tetlock, Edward Tufte, Richard Vadon, Matt

Vella, Jacob Weisberg, Tim Whiting, Patrick Wolfe, David Wootton, Andrew Wright, Frank Wynne, Ed Yong and Jason Zweig. There are more – many more. Thank you to everyone and apologies for all those who I have somehow missed.

In particular, thanks to the team at Wren and Rook: Kaltoun Yusuf, Laura Horsley, Pippi Grantham-Wright, Victoria Walsh and the incredible Ollie Mann for the way his illustrations have captured and transformed my ideas. And as always I am so grateful to my literary agent Sally Holloway.

Thank you to my children, Stella, Africa and Herbie, for helping me explore and explain some of the ideas in this book. And to Fran Monks; I'm not even going to try to count the ways I am grateful – they would fill another book.